Digital Leadership Framework

Digital Leadership Framework

Cultivating the Four Key Competencies

Amit Prabhu

BEP

BUSINESS EXPERT PRESS

Leader in applied, concise business books

Digital Leadership Framework: Cultivating the Four Key Competencies

First published in 2024 by
Business Expert Press, LLC
222 East 46th Street, New York, NY 10017
www.businessexpertpress.com

ISBN-13: 978-1-63742-591-6 (paperback)
ISBN-13: 978-1-63742-592-3 (e-book)

Business Expert Press Big Data, Business Analytics, and
Smart Technology Collection

First edition: 2024

10 9 8 7 6 5 4 3 2 1

To all the leaders who have inspired me with
their competence and character

Description

Digital transformation is the hallmark of digital era and the main driver behind digital leadership. Digital transformation is the new way of doing business with the help of latest emerging technologies. Digital leadership is the set of behaviors a leader must demonstrate in the digital age. The four key behaviors are learning new skills, connecting with people, leveraging data, and delivering results. To demonstrate them successfully, one must develop the following four key competencies:

1. Growth mindset
2. Empathy
3. Informed decision-making
4. Fast execution

Each of these competencies uniquely maps to a behavior:

Growth mindset enables learning.
Empathy enables people connections.
Informed decision-making enables leveraging data.
Fast execution enables delivering results.

This book contains a complete framework for digital leaders to develop these competencies. A digital leader could be an executive or a manager leading a team with decision-making responsibilities, or a transformation driver, or a change agent in an organization.

The success of this book lies in how effectively the leaders cultivate the competencies and apply them at their workplace. This book is not just about information…it's all about *transformation*!

Keywords

transformation; growth; mindset; empathy; informed; decision-making; fast; execution; brand; competencies; behaviors

Contents

Praise for Digital Leadership Framework

"Amit Prabhu helps you understand the new skills that digital leaders must master. Digital Leadership Framework *shows you how to pursue effective management and personal character development simultaneously, addressing the leadership challenges of our time."* —**Elisa Farri, Thinkers50 Radar Class of 2023 member, Author, Colead of Capgemini Invent's Management Lab, Harvard Business Review Contributor**

"A refreshing take on the digital conundrum and the consequent demands on leadership to successfully navigate enterprises through a complex transformation. Amit has creatively woven his real-world experience, an extensive network of sources, and academic research into a lucid and compelling narrative. Kudos." —**Aniruddho Basu, Executive Vice President, Mavenir**

"Amit Prabhu explains that driving change is essential for effectiveness. He emphasizes that this is particularly true in the current digital age, where leaders must navigate new expectations balancing risks, rewards, and skills." —**Arati Davis, Chief Operating Officer, Sweden-India Business Council, Advisory Committee Member at International WoMenX in Business for Ethical AI**

"Digital Leadership Framework is a practical guide for anyone working with digital transformation of organizations and finding out that good old management recipes no longer work in the digital age. The author insightfully builds a comprehensive framework interweaving competences, behaviors, and a suitable leadership style that will help firms succeed in the digital age. Importantly, the book is enriched by lively examples from organizations from different parts of the world. I will use this book for teaching in my course on project management." —**Katja Einola, Associate Professor, Department of Management and Organization, Stockholm School of Economics**

"Digital Leadership Framework *is a personal compass designed to help you lead effectively in times of groundbreaking technologies and shifting human behaviors, emphasizing the importance of growth mindset and empathy in making strategic decisions. The book offers a comprehensive journey to master the crucial skills for modern digital leadership, combining solid research with real-world applications and actionable exercises, to tackle the complex challenges of today's digital landscape.*" —**Emi Olausson Fourounjieva, Adviser, Transformational Coach for Leaders and Business Consultants, Founder and Host of the podcast "Digital Transformation for Humans"**

Introduction

In the digital age we are currently living in, customer needs change. Industry dynamics change. Business models change. Competence requirements change. Project parameters change. However, the leadership required to drive these changes has not changed much. Most leaders continue to drive digital transformation using the old predigital style of leadership. As per a recent study by McKinsey, 70 percent of digital transformation projects fail.[1] The main reason for failure is a lack of *digital leadership*.

In the predigital age:

- Leaders exercised power.
- Leaders were experts.
- Leaders mentored people.

The digital age demands new paradoxical leadership attributes where:

- Leaders exercise power yet empower.
- Leaders share yet seek expertise.
- Leaders mentor yet reverse mentor.

It is evident from the picture of the birds flying in v-like formation on the front cover of this book. The leader is the red bird, who has empowered the bird at the vertex of this formation to lead the flock. If it was the predigital era, the red bird would have been expected to be at the vertex leading others. An organization needs to adapt to these new attributes of digital leadership, which focuses on developing not only the right skillsets but also the right mindset.

In the predigital age, leaders exercised power. The corporate hierarchy was mostly rigid and top-down. Most of the decisions were taken by the executives. They issued directives to people telling them what to do and were less open to receiving inputs or feedback. They set high performance expectations for all and often micromanaged people.

Whereas, in the digital age, in addition to exercising power, leaders must empower. Empowering people to make decisions is a sign of trust and confidence. It motivates them, which in turn contributes to high performance levels and well-being. It also gives leaders some free time to focus on more complex business issues or customers. It does not mean that leaders completely give up their control and accountability. They should always be available to support people when faced with issues and facilitate solutions through their experience, network, and professional connections. They need to be involved in major decisions that have huge financial impact. Otherwise, for minor decisions, they can delegate the decision-making to their team.

In the predigital age, leaders were experts. They were supposed to have thorough knowledge about a product or a service and had a great influence on how a particular task had to be done. It was very much true in the 1990s and 2000s, when the world saw enormous growth in the IT industry that transformed every business and industry. It gave rise to many IT startups. Almost all the founders of these startups had technical backgrounds and were considered experts in their fields. It was also true for other industries such as banking, finance, healthcare, automotive, where an individual with years of vast industry knowledge and experience was promoted to the top ranks of a CEO or an executive in a firm.

In the digital age, in addition to sharing, leaders must seek knowledge and expertise. Digital transformation projects involve new digital technologies and new business practices never adopted nor implemented before. Thus, a leader may not have all the necessary expertise to deliver. A leader should be humble to admit that he/she does not know everything and should be courageous to step out of his/her comfort zone to learn more and ask for help from the experts. This sends out a positive message of collaborative learning in the organization motivating people to leverage knowledge from each other.

In the predigital age, leaders mentored people. Mentoring is a relationship between two individuals either within the same company, different companies in the same industry, or different companies in different industries, with the goal of professional and personal development. Mentors, who are experienced individuals, support and encourage their mentees, who are less experienced, by offering advice and suggestions to improve their skills and advance their careers.

Whereas, in the digital age, in addition to mentoring, leaders must reverse mentor. Most of the junior colleagues and fresh graduates in organizations today are millennials. They were born in the ending phase of the predigital era and grew up as teens in the digital era. Gadgets with screens are part of their everyday lives. They have the raw talent and fresh perspectives toward new digital technologies, which leaders should harness effectively through reverse mentoring.

The *digital* age is the era of digital transformation which began in the early 2010 decade. Before 2010 was the *predigital* age. The digital age saw a prominent rise of new digital businesses and the transformation of traditional businesses to digital ones driven by digital transformation technologies such as AI, automation, cloud, 5G, Internet of things (IoT), blockchain, data science and data analytics, gamification, virtual reality (VR)/augmented reality (AR)/extended reality (XR), metaverse, and so on. It is not that these technologies did not exist before 2010 and they appeared suddenly thereafter. Their research and development were ongoing much before 2010 and a few were launched in the market too. It was just that in the digital era, the businesses began to be commercially aware and rapidly adopted them through the development of various user applications.

The main difference between traditional and digital businesses is that digital businesses normally have *3S*:

- Scale
- Scope
- Speed

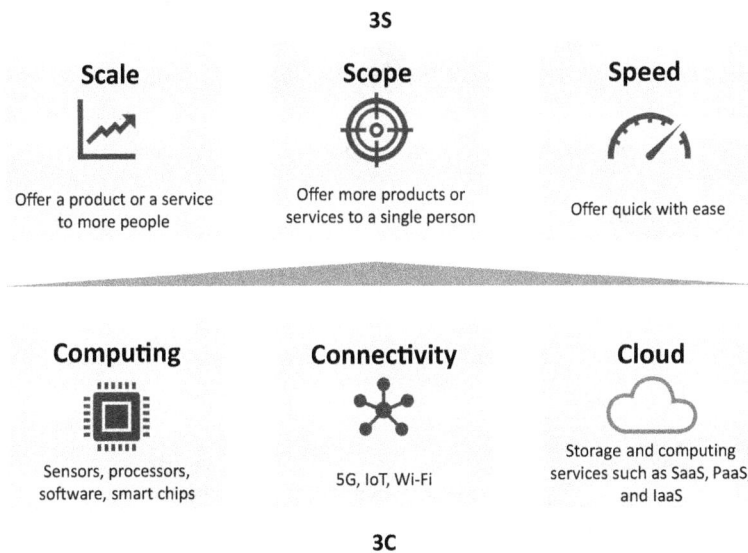

3S

Scale	Scope	Speed
Offer a product or a service to more people	Offer more products or services to a single person	Offer quick with ease

Computing	Connectivity	Cloud
Sensors, processors, software, smart chips	5G, IoT, Wi-Fi	Storage and computing services such as SaaS, PaaS, and IaaS

3C

Figure I.1 3S and 3C

These are enabled by *3C*:

- Computing
- Connectivity
- Cloud

Scale implies offering a single product or a service to multiple customers. *Scope* implies offering multiple products or services to a single customer based on its preferences. *Speed* implies offering products or services quickly with ease and affordability. *Computing* power grew exponentially with the development of smaller chipsets, and recently with quantum computing. Technologies such as 4G and 5G improved *connectivity* significantly with higher data speeds. There was a paradigm shift in how we store data and information with the advent of *cloud*.

Digital transformation is a new way of doing business with the help of latest emerging technologies. The new way of doing business implies driving changes in:

- Customer engagement
- Internal operations
- Corporate culture

Customer engagement is how we interact with and manage relationships with our customers. *Internal operations* are the daily activities we need to do to keep our business running. *Corporate culture* refers to values, beliefs, and behaviors that determine how a company's employees and

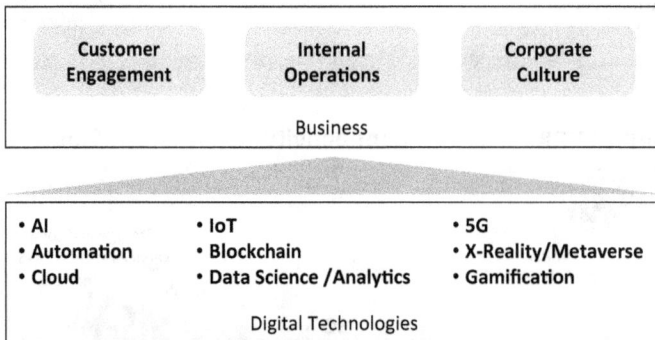

Customer Engagement	Internal Operations	Corporate Culture
Business		

• AI • Automation • Cloud	• IoT • Blockchain • Data Science /Analytics	• 5G • X-Reality/Metaverse • Gamification
Digital Technologies		

Figure I.2 Digital transformation

management interact, perform, and handle business transactions.[2] The digital technologies include AI, automation, cloud, 5G, IoT, blockchain, data science and data analytics, gamification, VR/AR/XR, metaverse, etc. If you just change the way you do business without using any of the digital technologies, it is not digital transformation. Or, if you just adopt digital technologies but stick to your old ways of doing business, it is still not digital transformation. Digital transformation means transforming business using digital technologies. It has a business and a technology component to it.

Customer needs change. In the predigital age, customers wanted better quality of products or services, preferred commoditized or generalized products or services, and preferred ownership of resources. However, in the digital age, customers more than quality want better experiences with products or services. Instead of generalization, they want personalization. And instead of ownership, they want shared access to resources.

Experiences	Personalization	Shared access
From product or services to better customer experiences	Personalized interactions at various touch points in a customer's journey	Transition from ownership to access

New business models

Figure I.3 Customer wants in digital age

An example of a better experience is NikeID or *Nike by You*, which allows customers to create a unique shoe design as per their choice. An example of personalization is YouTube, which recommends videos to users based on preferences and past viewership. An example of shared access is Share Now, a German carsharing company, formed from the merger between Car2Go and DriveNow. Customers using Share Now don't have to pay for parking, fuel, or insurance. All the rates are all-inclusive and are as flexible as pay-per-minute. They can drive whenever they want. This is unlike the car rentals where they have to pick up and drop off within specific opening hours. If they see a Share Now vehicle, they just need to hop in and drive. Also, they can park their cars anywhere within the city.[3]

Industry dynamics change. In the predigital age, the industry landscape or value chain was static. There was a clear distinction between customers, suppliers, and competitors. But in the digital age, the industry landscape is dynamic. A customer in one market can be a supplier in another, a competitor can be a collaborator, and a vendor can be a partner. For example, in the telecommunications industry, in the early 2000s, during the 3G era, the telco vendors offered products and services to the telco operators to provide an efficient network infrastructure for their individual and enterprise end-customers. But currently, in the digital era of 5G, the roles are reversed in some cases. The telco vendors are directly approaching the end-customers such as manufacturing industries, airports, healthcare, utilities, for solutions such as private 5G networks. The telco operators in this value chain are playing an important role of suppliers providing connectivity.

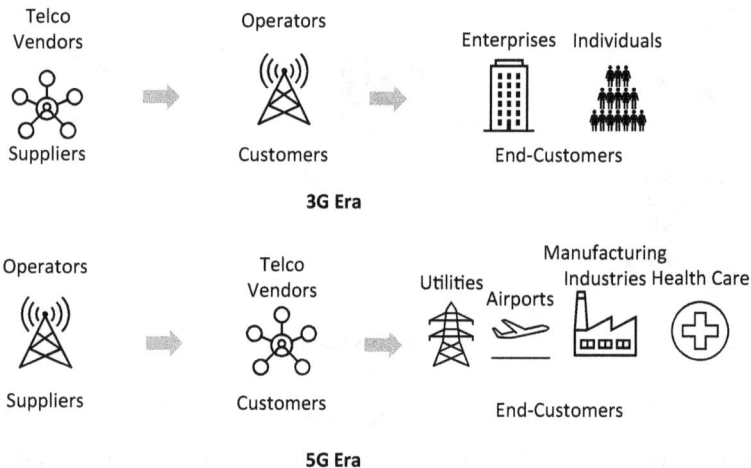

Figure I.4 Static and dynamic value chains

Business models change. In the predigital age, the business models were traditional or linear, where one typically played the role of a manufacturer, supplier, retailer, or consumer. Whereas, in the digital age, most of the business models are platform based, where one can play multiple roles such as owner, orchestrator, seller, and buyer. An owner is the controller

Manufacturer   Supplier   Retailer   Consumer

Traditional Business Model

Owner

Platform

Buyer →   ← Seller

Orchestrator

Platform based Business Model

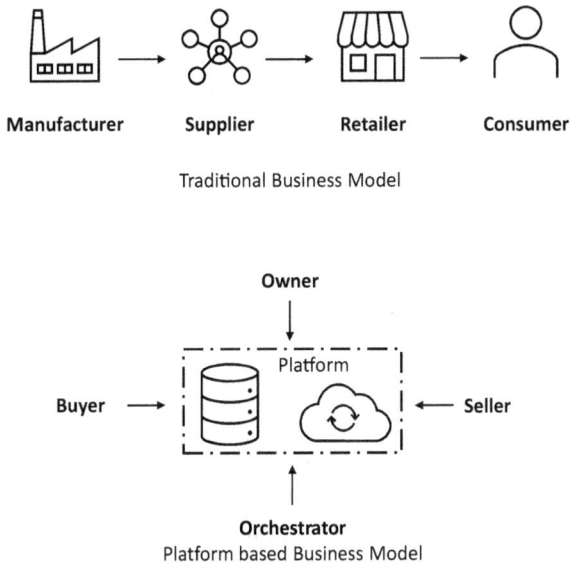

Figure I.5 Traditional and platform based business models

of the platform who sets business rules and policies and decides who may participate in the platform and in what way. An orchestrator facilitates the platform. A seller creates offerings on the platform. A buyer purchases the offerings.

Android is a platform. Google is the owner, handset manufacturers are the orchestrators, app developers are the sellers, and app users are the buyers.

Uber is a platform. Uber is the owner, vehicle owners are the orchestrators, vehicle drivers are the sellers, and Uber customers are the buyers. Vehicle owners can be vehicle drivers and play the dual role of orchestrators and sellers.

Airbnb is a platform. Airbnb is the owner, property owners are the orchestrators and sellers, and guests are the buyers.

Competence requirements change. In the predigital age, the top IT competencies were coding languages (C, C++, Java), database administration, unix, linux, data warehousing, TCP/IP networking, quality assurance, testing, and website development. In the digital age, the top IT competencies are python programming, cloud, cybersecurity, kubernetes and terraform, continuous integration / continuous deployment (CI/CD), automation, AI, machine learning (ML), DevOps, data science, digital marketing, and UI/UX design. There is a shortage of these skills in the market, and many organizations have initiated upskilling and reskilling programs to develop them internally.

Project parameters change. The digital transformation projects of the digital age are more complex, costly, risky, and uncertain than the normal IT projects of the predigital age. They involve digital technologies with the objective of creating new ways of working for the business. For example, an activity that includes designing a simple web portal hosting online learning courses is a normal IT project. But when you add data analytics to the web portal to track user behavior and provide business insights such as how students learn, how many courses they enroll, how many courses they complete, reviews they provide, and when you add AI to recommend courses to students based on their preferences and online behavior, it becomes a digital transformation project. A survey was conducted for around 150 IT managers, who had experience in delivering both normal IT and digital transformation projects. They were asked to provide a rating on a scale of 1 to 10 for the following project parameters:

- Complexity
- Uncertainty
- Costs
- Delayed timelines
- Competence shortage
- Risks

It was observed that a digital transformation project compared to a normal IT project is:

- 3.5 times more complex
- 4 times more uncertain
- 1.4 times more costly
- 2 times slower
- 7 times more competence-short
- 2.6 times more risky

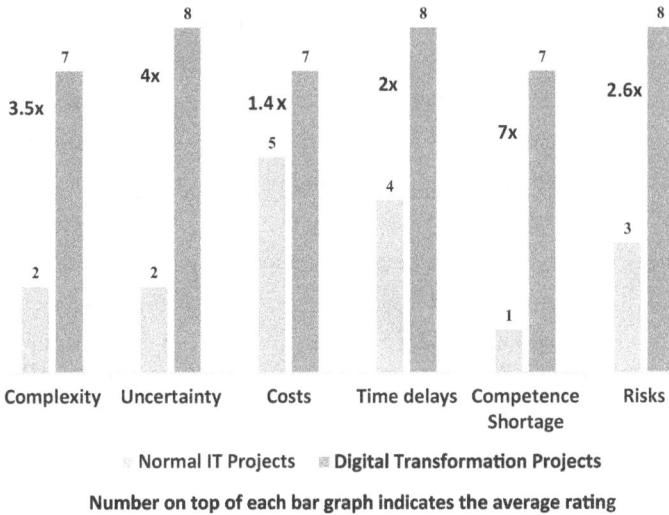

Figure I.6 Comparison between normal IT and digital transformation projects

A global multinational firm based in Nordics wanted to explore the benefits of using robotic process automation (RPA) to automate its business processes using bots. The CTO entrusted the responsibility to Alan (name changed), the head of strategy execution, to carry out a feasibility analysis. Alan onboarded one of his trusted direct reports in this activity. After six weeks of market analysis and research, Alan presented a proposal to the executive leadership team about the creation of a new automation unit in the organization. The proposal was accepted, and Alan became the unit head. There was a U.S.$1 million operational budget approved with the aim to reduce costs worth U.S.$5 million over the next two years. Soon the team expanded rapidly. Most of the team comprised people with prior IT experience. It was an attractive place to be for many employees from their career perspectives. Most of them did not have any competence in using the technology before. The firm had to seek help from external vendors. The contract was awarded to one of the top RPA vendors. With the support from the vendor, the firm drafted a strategy focusing on the target areas for piloting. The supply function was chosen for piloting test cases as it had lots of administrative, repetitive, and manual processes that were adding costs. After a few weeks, the first bot was created to automate the order tracking system. The pilot was successful. A few more proofs of concept (PoCs) were developed. To scale up, many bots were introduced in the system. Soon the 100th bot was deployed. There were celebrations and articles in the corporate newsletter. However, this did not last long.

Around the same time, the IT team commenced a modernization program where they began upgrading and updating most of the systems. This resulted in the operational failure of the bots. The automation team faced huge escalations, which were difficult for them to handle. The problem with the bots was that they were not intelligent enough to detect and adapt to the changes in the IT environment. Every single bot action had to be programmed. Lots of manpower had to be deployed to troubleshoot the bots. Instead of reducing the costs, the expenses of running and maintaining the bots kept on piling up.

Another cost contributor was that the underlying IT infrastructure of the company was fragmented. It had different siloed islands of software, tools, and systems, which lacked a seamless data transfer. The bots were introduced in different siloed islands and were running at almost half of their fully optimized capacity. If they had implemented the best practice of creating a *data lake*, an environment that enables a smooth and seamless flow of data, few bots would have been sufficient to manage the operations. It would have significantly reduced the costs.

Alan and his team were focused on meeting the cost targets and did not connect well with the group IT experts and other business stakeholders in the organization and ran the project pretty much standalone without proper feedback from them. They relied on the RPA vendor for the automation competence and did not invest much to develop one internally. Many decisions were taken instinctively without leveraging the available data and information. Most of the senior managers and leaders in the automation unit had prior IT experience from the predigital age. They brought in the same old leadership styles and outlooks that did not match the risky and unpredictable project environment.

This is the problem with most leaders today. Most of them have the experience of handling predictable outcomes and performances. They assume that the future is going to be very much like the past. They lack knowledge and experience of new digital technologies, and thus, are unable to assess their business impacts. Most of them are unwilling to adapt to the demands and expectations of the digital age and change their leadership styles accordingly. Organizations too are structured and designed to manage predictable performances. The need for consistent and unsurprising results gets incorporated into every aspect of the enterprise—the formal structures, culture, systems, processes, norms, decision-making criteria, and habits, which makes it very difficult to adapt and manage uncertainty. That's why they fail.

After interviewing several leaders from different companies across the globe, I discovered that there are four key behaviors essential to handling the unpredictability and uncertainty of digital transformation projects better and helping them excel as effective digital leaders:

1. Learning new skills
2. Connecting with people
3. Leveraging data
4. Delivering results

The four key competencies are not new and most leaders are aware of them. Though there are few books written on digital leadership, there is not a single one that discusses these competencies and provides a framework on how to cultivate them. Neither there is much information available on the Internet.

In this book, I have addressed this gap by providing frameworks for digital leaders to cultivate these competencies. It contains six chapters. Chapter 1 explains the digital leadership framework. From chapters 2 to 5, each of the digital leadership competencies is discussed in detail. Chapter 6 contains the practical application of the frameworks. The readers can either read the book sequentially or jump to any chapter from one to five, as per their needs and interests. Go to chapter 6 to continue reading the relevant sections only after you have read at least one of the earlier chapters.

Cultivating these competencies would enable one to demonstrate the earlier stated paradoxical attributes too. Empathy and fast execution would drive empowerment. Growth mindset and informed decision-making would facilitate the seeking of knowledge and expertise. And empathy and growth mindset would encourage mentoring and reverse mentoring.

This book is not a sequel to my earlier one, *Digital Strategy Framework: A Practical Guide for Business Incumbents*—rather, it supplements it. My earlier one provides a framework to create and execute a digital strategy and apply it at the organizational level. This book provides a framework to cultivate the four key digital competencies and apply them at an individual level. A digital leader can be an executive, a manager leading a team with decision-making responsibilities, a transformation driver, or a change agent in an organization.

The success of this book lies in how effectively the leaders cultivate the competencies and apply them at their workplace. This book is not just about information…it's all about *transformation*!

CHAPTER 1

Digital Leadership Framework

Digital leadership is the set of behaviors a leader must demonstrate in the digital age. The main driver behind digital leadership is digital transformation. Figure 1.1 shows the digital leadership framework.

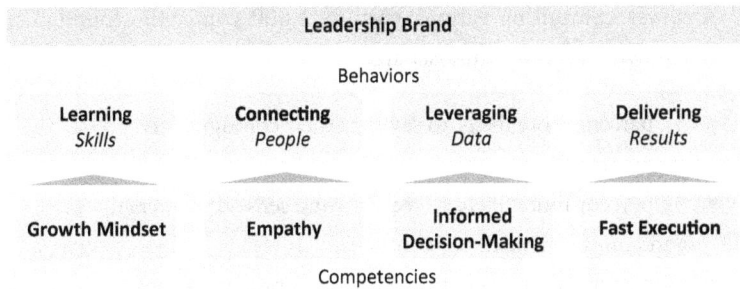

Leadership Brand

Behaviors

Learning	**Connecting**	**Leveraging**	**Delivering**
Skills	*People*	*Data*	*Results*

Growth Mindset	**Empathy**	**Informed Decision-Making**	**Fast Execution**

Competencies

Figure 1.1 Digital leadership framework

The top of the framework contains the leadership brand, which is shaped by the underlying behaviors: learning new skills, connecting with people, leveraging data, and delivering results, and key competencies: *growth mindset, empathy, informed decision-making,* and *fast execution.* The four key competencies map to the four essential behaviors. These behaviors also map across all three areas of digital transformation: customer engagement, internal operations, and corporate culture.

Competencies

Growth Mindset

Growth mindset is a frame of mind where people believe that their skills are not inbuilt but can be developed through effort and dedication. This

Top 4 Essential Behaviors of a Digital Leader

Customer
Engagement

Digital
Transformation   **Internal**   **Learning**   **People**   **Leveraging**   **Delivering**
Areas   *Operations*   new Skills   Connections   Data   Results

Corporate
Culture

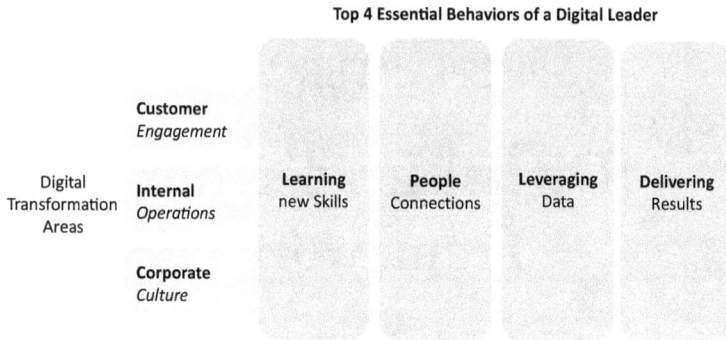

Figure 1.2 Behaviors and transformation areas mapping

ignites a passion for learning and builds resilience, that are essential for
great accomplishments.

A survey comprising various Fortune 1,000 companies found that
employees with a growth mindset are:[1]

- 47 percent more likely to say that their colleagues are
  trustworthy.
- 34 percent more likely to feel a strong sense of ownership
  and commitment to the company.
- 65 percent more likely to say that the company supports
  risk-taking.
- 49 percent more likely to say that the company fosters
  innovation.

Therefore, a digital leader must cultivate a growth mindset.

Empathy

Empathy is the ability to understand other people's emotions. It is about
understanding what others think, feel, and will (desire).

Employees describe an empathetic leader as someone who is transparent, fair, and follows through on actions. The top five qualities employees
look for in him/her are as follows:

- Openness and transparency
- Fairness

- Follow-through on actions
- Encouraging others to share their opinions
- Trust to handle difficult conversations

A lack of empathy at the workplace has caused many employees to leave their jobs, which is considered to be a possible contributor to the *great resignation* in the years 2021 to 2022. Over half (58 percent) of employees left because they didn't feel valued by their managers, nearly half (48 percent) left because they didn't feel a sense of belonging, and more than a third (37 percent) of employees left due to the difficulty in connecting with colleagues.[2] Therefore, a digital leader must cultivate empathy.

Informed Decision-Making

Informed decision-making involves making decisions based on accurate, reliable, and relevant information. It involves gathering and analyzing data, considering multiple perspectives, and using critical thinking skills to evaluate options and make the best choice.

One should be able to access and leverage the right type of data. The number of decisions to be made has soared, and there is too much data available. Here are some facts from the study of more than 14,000 business leaders across 17 countries:[3]

- 74 percent said that the number of decisions they make every day has increased 10× over the last three years, and as they try to make these decisions, 78 percent are getting loaded with more data from more sources than ever before.
- 86 percent said that the volume of data is making decisions in their personal and professional lives much more complicated and 59 percent admit that they face a decision dilemma— not knowing what decision to make—more than once every single day.
- 35 percent do not know which data or sources to trust.
- 70 percent have given up on decision-making being overwhelmed by the data.

- 85 percent of people say that this inability to make decisions is having a negative impact on their quality of life. It is causing spikes in anxiety (36 percent), missed opportunities (33 percent), and unnecessary spending (29 percent).
- As a result, 93 percent have changed the way they make decisions over the last three years. Also, 39 percent now only listen to sources they trust, and 29 percent rely solely on gut feelings.

Most of the corporate decisions made by leaders and managers are biased. One executive recruiter says:

Executives make up their minds about whether they like a candidate in the first 20 seconds and spend the next half-hour justifying their decision. It's called the "halo effect." Once you have formed an opinion, you only see what you want to see.

Another headhunter says:

I can spend endless hours screening candidates and culling resumes that fit the criteria I have painstakingly developed with a client. And managers will still hire the person with the right "chemistry" even if they don't fit the criteria at all. They fall in love with a candidate and that's it.[4]

Biased decision-making can have negative implications such as inequity and discrimination, lower morale and productivity, missed opportunities, lack of innovation, talent drain, resistance to change, and stifled collaboration. Therefore, a digital leader must cultivate informed decision-making.

Fast Execution

Fast execution is the ability to take rapid actions in both certain and uncertain environments. It is more challenging to act in unpredictable conditions than predictable ones because, as said before, leaders are more accustomed to handling definite results and outcomes.

During the pandemic year of 2021, a survey of nearly 1,000 global business and technology professionals was conducted to understand how organizations are responding to change and what is making them success-ful.[5] The focus was on the speed and quality of outcomes. The companies were divided into three categories:

- Leaders (forward-moving and proactive to change)
- Challengers (forward-moving but reactive to change)
- Laggards (slower, often stalled)

The results revealed a significant gap between them:

- Leaders were overcoming barriers and adapting more quickly to change than their competitors.
- Leaders were three times more likely to exceed financial targets and strategic objectives than challengers.
- 90 percent of leaders wanted to make decisions and execute them faster. This was a percentage much higher than challengers and laggards.
- Challengers and laggards were showing less resolve to execute faster.
- Leaders were investing more in improving processes and technology to reap more benefits such as customer satisfaction, employee satisfaction, and new customer acquisition.

One can have the best plan, best team, and best product, but unless one takes action, nothing happens. Therefore, a digital leader must culti-vate fast execution.

These four competencies will be discussed in more detail in the upcoming chapters.

Behaviors

After interviewing several leaders across different industries on what behaviors are expected from them for better efficiency and performance, the following four were ranked top: learning new skills, connecting with people, leveraging data, and delivering results.

Learning New Skills

Digital transformation has given rise to new jobs that demand new digital skillsets. Hence, learning new digital skills is very important. Most organizations find it difficult to find people with such skills and competencies for the job. As per a report by the World Economic Forum, there is a global shortage of digital skills, which could mean 85 million jobs would remain unfilled by 2030.[6] Businesses in all sectors need to have a long-term strategy for developing them. If the right competence cannot be acquired externally, it is best to build it internally through upskilling and reskilling programs.

PricewaterhouseCoopers (PwC) embarked on a strategy named *Digital Fitness*, which aimed at developing their digital skills across different domains such as data analytics, AI, automation, blockchain, and design. They created a digital fitness app, which the employees could download on their phones. It provided them with a personal assessment of their digital acumen and a recommendation on the tools and learning resources, they need to fill their competence gap and make improvements. It provided a customized learning path, which helped in workforce planning and skills development strategies. For those employees desiring to further develop their digital skills, a *Digital Accelerator* program was created with support from the PwC leadership. The employees all across the organization were asked to apply for the program that had a competitive selection process. In 2018, around 1,000 out of 3,500 applicants were selected for the program. They were known as the *Accelerators*. They were offered a facility to rapidly deepen their skills in digital technologies by learning a variety of self-service tools and coding languages and applying these skills across the PwC business. A personal development path was carved for each Accelerator. The work responsibilities were reduced for them, which allowed them to free up time to learn, collaborate, and execute. They had to work full time with clients for at least two years in this role, where they could practically apply these skills learned. These Accelerators showed some remarkable results. Through intelligent automation and AI, they could reduce the tasks that required 1,000+ hours to a few minutes or even seconds, creating capacity for PwC employees and their clients to focus on other high-priority tasks. Another important benefit of the program was that it was successful in creating a community of highly passionate and driven tech-savvy problem solvers within the organization, who were strongly connected personally and drove accelerated learning through knowledge sharing among peers.[7]

There is a company in the Nordics whose learning and development (L&D) team has started a business book club to encourage everyone to read and learn. Even some of the top executives are part of the club. The club has three groups: heavy readers, medium readers, and lite readers, who are expected to finish a book within one week, two weeks, and four weeks, respectively, from a predefined list of books relevant and important to the business. At the end of their respective weeks, the different groups meet and discuss the important points, lessons learned, and how can they apply them to their business. This book club has enabled better connections and communications between the employees at different hierarchical levels and brought out new business ideas for implementation.

To enable digital learning, almost all organizations have created an L&D function. This can be an independent function. But in most cases, it falls under the human resources (HR). During the pandemic, a round table discussion was organized by Digiculum, a learning ecosystem orchestration management firm, based in Stockholm, Sweden, for all the L&D drivers and managers in the Nordics from different industries. The topic was to understand the challenges faced by L&D in implementing learning in their organizations and the solutions to overcome them. After sufficient brainstorming, the following were the challenges identified:

1. Linking learning to business objectives and measuring impact
2. Support and buy-in from top leaders
3. Breaking silos across different teams
4. Accessibility to the right learning assets
5. Different perspectives to learning at different levels in the corporate hierarchy

6. Incorporate learning into daily jobs
7. Not sure where to start from
8. Keeping employees motivated to learn
9. Show tangible results to business stakeholders
10. Relevancy of content
11. Life cycle management of the content
12. Priority mismatch between stakeholders
13. No long-term learning vision
14. Unwillingness to experiment with new ways of learning

The Digiculum team then prepared a survey comprising the above 14 challenges and sent it to more than 500 participants across different companies. The respondents were asked to rank the top five challenges in the order of high to low business impact.
Following was the outcome:

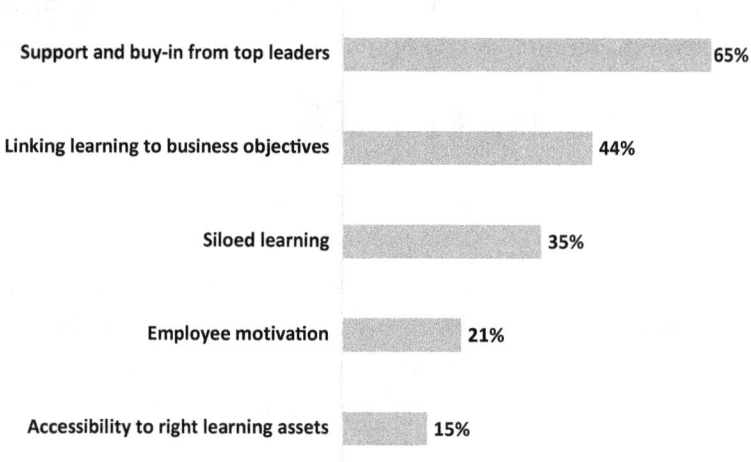

Figure 1.3 Top 5 L&D challenges in implementing learning

Out of 531 respondents,

- 65 percent considered support and buy-in from top leaders as rank 1.
- 44 percent considered linking learning to business objectives as rank 2.
- 35 percent considered siloed learning as rank 3.

- 21 percent considered keeping employees motivated to learn as rank 4.
- 15 percent considered accessibility to the right learning assets as rank 5.

After a few weeks, another round table conference was held with the L&D drivers and managers to deep dive into the challenges and understand why it was difficult to seek support and buy-in from top leaders. Following were the responses:

- Lack of funds / learning budget.
- Learning not a top priority for leaders.
- Lack of mindset and attitude toward learning.

Another survey was conducted by Digiculum to understand the top reason for the lack of support and buy-in from leaders.

Following was the outcome:

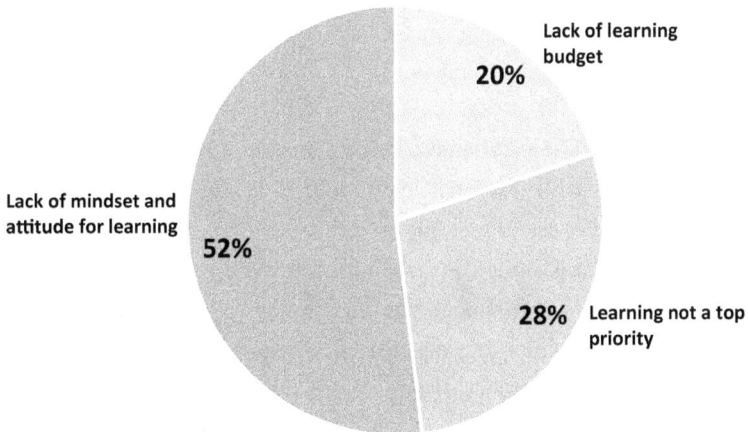

Figure 1.4 Reasons for lack of buy-in support from leaders

Out of 423 respondents,

- 20 percent voted for lack of a learning budget.
- 28 percent voted for learning not a top priority.
- 52 percent voted for lack of mindset and attitude for learning.

In other words, they voted for the lack of *growth mindset*.

Connecting with People

Digital transformation projects need collaboration among the team members. It is important that people who mostly work in a hybrid environment feel connected with each other to facilitate mutual trust and sharing of knowledge and information.

Before the pandemic, at Fujitsu, a Japanese multinational technology and business solutions provider, an internal survey was conducted on flexible working environments. More than 74 percent of the employees preferred to work from office. During the pandemic, around 80,000 of Fujitsu's workforce was working from home. Toward the end of the pandemic, the same survey was conducted again:

- 15 percent of employees said they wanted to work from office.
- 30 percent of employees said they wanted to continue working from home.
- 55 percent of employees favored a mix of home and office— the hybrid model.

They reasoned that around two hours, which goes waste in commuting could be better utilized for education, training, and with family. As per a global survey by ADP Research Institute in 2021, 64 percent of workers said they would consider looking for a new job if they were to return to office full-time.[8] Like employees at Fujitsu, many employees from different companies across the globe feel that the hybrid model would work the best. It is a once-in-a-lifetime opportunity for business leaders to reset work using a hybrid model. If done correctly, it would make the work lives of employees more purposeful, productive, and flexible.[9]

One of the biggest challenges for a digital leader is to connect people with each other and with the organization and to manage their expectations by keeping them engaged in the hybrid workplace. Most business leaders were concerned that remote work setup during the pandemic and hybrid work setup postpandemic was undermining the corporate culture and endangering the people connections, which are important for the growth and profitability of the company. As per a study by Gartner in 2022, only 25 percent of the remote or hybrid knowledge workers feel connected to their company's culture.[10] Therefore, it is important that people connect at the workplace for their professional and psychological well-being. Hybrid work carries a risk of creating a *dominant class* of those who feel they are strongly committed and connected to the organization and an *underclass* of those who feel alienated and disconnected, not only from work but also from social events and activities that bonds employees more closely to the organization.[11] A study found that despite 85 percent of HR leaders agreeing that employees should feel connected at work, only 31 percent of organizations have actively addressed connection challenges.[12]

A survey was conducted by Digiculum on what would make people feel more connected to work in a hybrid environment. Following was the response:

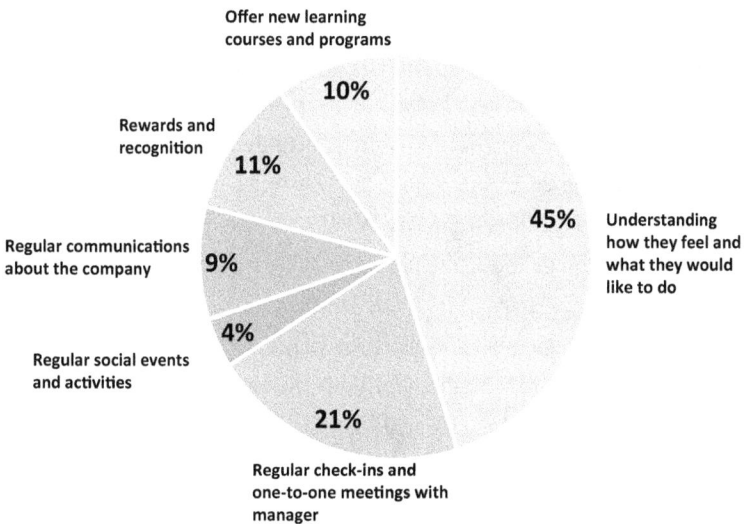

Figure 1.5 What would make people connected to work in a hybrid environment

Out of 323 respondents,

- 4 percent said regular social events and activities.
- 21 percent said regular check-ins and one-to-one meetings with manager.
- 10 percent said offer new learning courses and programs.

- 9 percent said regular communications about the company.
- 11 percent said rewards and recognition.
- 45 percent said understanding how they feel and what they would like to do.

In other words, they wanted *empathy*.

Leveraging Data

The digital transformation projects involve working with and generating lots of data. This data, if used efficiently, can provide real-time metrics and insights to an organization, which its competitors may not have. It can help to make important decisions, improve efficiency, and enhance customer experience.

For example, at WeWork, the largest provider of office spaces for start-ups, small-to-medium-sized businesses, and big enterprise customers with more than 1,000 employees, large amount of data was collected from its 400,000+ members. This data was used to understand how the existing workplaces can be customized and the new ones can be built. A study conducted by CB Insights regarding WeWork showed that the sensors and various measurement tools, including facial recognition software can be used to monitor the usage of its office spaces. These tools provide detailed data, such as how members adjust their desks, which areas of the office experience the most foot traffic, and even the level of focus exhibited by members during meetings. To enable this, WeWork acquired an architecture technology firm Case Inc. in 2015 and a construction management firm Field Lens in 2017. Case Inc. offered predictive modeling for designing future buildings in three-dimensions (3D). Field Lens offered technology for construction stakeholders to manage sites in real time on their phones. The building information modeling (BIM) process of Case Inc. increased efficiency between 15 and 20 percent, saving 10 percent of building costs. Machine learning technology was used by researchers at WeWork that reaped data on existing building layouts and conference room usage to figure out how many meeting rooms to build. This improved the room usage estimation accuracy by 40 percent. A single extra desk added U.S.$80,000 in revenue over 10 years. Through a partnership with Factual, a location data provider, WeWork could rate locations based on proximity to amenities such as shops, restaurants, bars, and hotels. It helped them realize a 95 percent increase in locations from 2016 to 2017, which significantly shortened the time between identifying, opening, and filling a new building with tenants.[13]

Unlike WeWork, it is generally observed that data is not leveraged fully by the businesses. According to a recent survey released by Gartner, despite 44 percent of data and analytics teams increased its size in 2022, only 44 percent of team leaders said their teams are providing value to their organization.[14] The common challenges that businesses face when leveraging data are as follows:[15]

- Overcoming resistance to change—Many businesses are used to making decisions based on intuition or experience, rather than data. As a result, they show resistance to adopting new processes or tools for collecting and analyzing data.
- Finding the right talent to manage and analyze data—Data analysis requires specialized skills and knowledge in statistics, machine learning, and programming. Businesses may struggle to find individuals with the right combination of technical skills and business acumen to effectively leverage data.
- Identifying the right data to use—With so much data available, businesses may struggle to identify which data are relevant and useful for their specific needs. Additionally, businesses must ensure that the data they collect is accurate, consistent, and compliant with data privacy regulations.
- Accessing the right data—Most of the data within the organization are available in silos, confined to different tools, systems, teams, and functions, making it less fluid. It is very difficult to secure access to the right type of data.

A survey was conducted by Digiculum on the topmost benefit of leveraging data through data analytics, where the respondents had to select between the following choices:[16]

- Improved decision-making
- Increased efficiency and productivity
- Enhanced customer experience
- Improved risk management
- Competitive advantage

Following was the outcome:

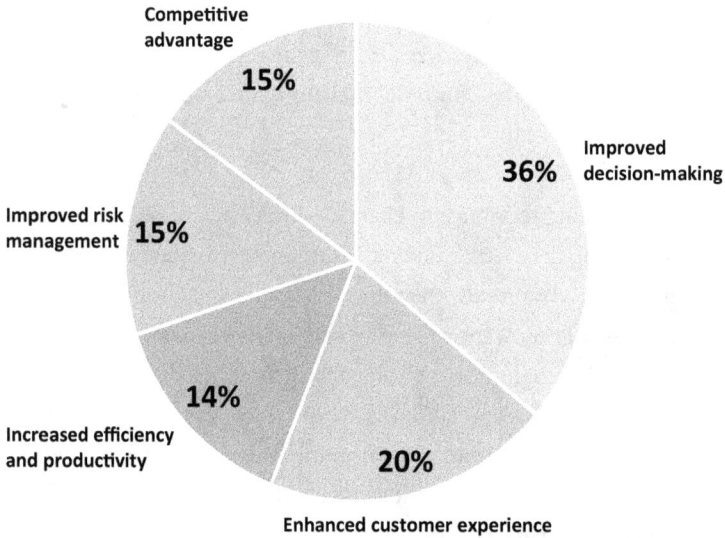

Figure 1.6 Benefits of leveraging data through data analytics

Out of 201 respondents,

- 14 percent said increased efficiency and productivity.
- 20 percent said enhanced customer experience.
- 15 percent said improved risk management.
- 15 percent said competitive advantage.
- 36 percent said improved decision-making.

In other words, they opted for informed decision-making.

Delivering Results

Digital transformation projects are generally long term with a span of three to five years. It can take a while before your team can see some tangible results. It can impact its morale and affect the overall performance. To avoid this, a good leader should continuously deliver results. He or she should break the big project phase into smaller phases or milestones and focus on achieving them. In other words, a leader should focus on quick wins. This can boost the team's morale, get people excited, and create value for the customers.

In a survey conducted on high-performing leaders, one attribute stood out—a strong focus on results. In fact, most of them had managed to secure a quick win—a new and visible contribution to the success of the business made early in their tenure. Those who had achieved a quick win scored on average nearly 20 percent higher on performance than those who hadn't. A quick win serves as an important confirmation for management to validate their decision regarding a promotion, for team members to assess their confidence in their new manager, and for peers to gauge the arrival of an equal in their group.[17]

A good example where a quick win is applicable is cloud migration. Most of the large business incumbents across the globe have begun the digital transformation projects of migrating their information technology (IT) applications to cloud—either public or private. The number of IT applications in the case of large organizations is huge, around or more than 300 approximately. Before the migration work begins, there is a prestudy that decides which IT applications to migrate and what is the right strategy. There is a 6R migration strategy that is currently popular:

- Retain
- Retire
- Rehost
- Replatform
- Replace
- Rearchitect

If the migration of an application does not make sense for your team now, then you can *retain* and decide moving to cloud later. If an application does not meet the business objectives, it is best to *retire* it instead of moving to cloud. In *rehost*, an application is moved to cloud as-is without making any changes to the application code. In *replatform*, an application is moved to cloud but on a new platform with some minor changes to the code. In *replace*, you are replacing your current application with a new cloud-based or a software-as-a-service (SaaS) product. In *rearchitect*, an application is moved to cloud with major changes to its architecture, platform, and underlying code.

The best practice used by the cloud migration project manager is to deliver fast results or secure quick wins by rehosting, which involves migrating the easy *lift and shift* applications, also called the low-hanging fruits. The costs of rehosting are less compared to the other strategies. By moving them first, the team gets a better understanding of the new cloud environment, known as the landing zone, allowing them to plan the migrations of complex applications better. These quick wins provide a good learning experience to new team members or those having less experience on cloud, which helps to boost their morale and confidence.

A digital transformation project faces longer delays than usual, making it difficult to secure quick wins. A report in 2020 found that an average digital transformation project can cost enterprises an average of U.S.\$27.5 million.[18] A recent survey of 200 IT decision makers revealed that IT teams are struggling to deliver them in a timely manner. With delays lasting five months on average, 88 percent of IT decision makers are paying up to £20,200 a day, or just over £3 million.[19]

A survey was conducted by Digiculum for the employees working on digital transformation projects across different industries, where the respondents had to select the top reason for delays in delivering results from the following:

- Inability to take quick actions
- Legacy systems and integration challenges
- Shortage of skills and talent
- Budget constraints
- Lack of collaboration across enterprise
- Lack of transformation priorities

Following was the outcome:

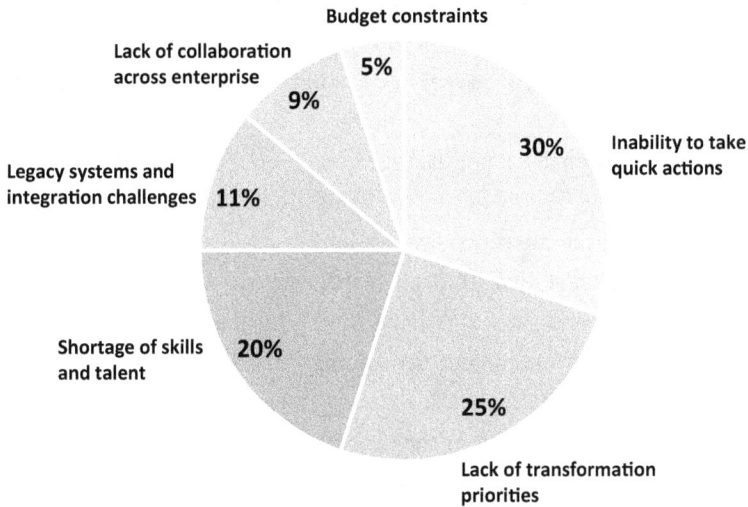

Figure 1.7 Reasons for delay in delivering results

Out of 488 respondents,

- 11 percent said legacy systems and integration challenges.
- 20 percent said shortage of skills and talent.
- 5 percent said budget constraints.
- 9 percent said lack of collaboration across enterprise.
- 25 percent said lack of transformation priorities.
- 30 percent said inability to take quick actions.

In other words, they voted for a lack of *fast execution*.

Leadership Brand

Leadership brand is the perception people have about you as a leader. It is very important to have good branding, as it helps to build trust and credibility with your team and with your customers, which is an important requirement for a successful business. Branding is something that people will remember you for a long. A strong and authentic leadership branding is built on one's values, which run deep within us. A leader might fake a branding. But it may not last long. In good times, when everything is nice and smooth, it may not be exposed. But in turbulent and uncertain times, the real nature of a leader becomes visible. One starts noticing the difference in the behaviors. A brand that is based on good values will stand strong in the face of adversities. People may not necessarily agree with the decisions you make but would certainly respect you for the values you stand for.

Recently, Mohan (name changed) was promoted to the head of operations in the Nordic healthcare company he had been for 10 years. He was excited about this new position. He had plans for increasing growth and profitability. The top management had high expectations from him. However, he didn't have good leadership branding. He was perceived as a controlling and demanding leader, to the point of being ruthless and impatient, when it came to driving change. His team was concerned about his arrival in the new role. Initially, it was very difficult for Mohan to connect with his team. There was very little trust and motivation. It took Mohan a lot of effort to rebrand his leadership style.

Some people believe that a leadership brand cannot be changed. They are wrong. It is possible to rebrand. In fact, the ability to readapt one's existing branding to fit the digital age is the mark of a successful digital leader.

The six popular and widely accepted leadership styles are as follows:

1. Autocratic
2. Affiliative
3. Democratic
4. Delegative
5. Pacesetting
6. Supportive
    1. Autocratic: It is a style where leaders assert authority and control over subordinates and demand unquestionable obedience from them. These leaders normally make decisions without seeking inputs and enough consultation from the team. This style is rarely effective and can lead to low morale and job satisfaction. It is useful in crisis, where quick decisions must be made. It is also referred to as an authoritarian, coercive, or commanding style.
    2. Affiliative: It is a style where leaders strive to emotionally connect with the team. This builds trust and fosters a sense of belonging.

It is effective during stressful situations, where an affiliative leader can boost low morale, improve communication, and create a harmonious work environment. The downside of the style is that constant praise and nurturing can cause performance issues to be overlooked.

3. Democratic: It is a style where leaders strive to seek consensus and are constantly asking for input from their team. They appreciate the knowledge, skills, and diversity everyone brings. These leaders are good listeners, and they build confidence in their leadership by utilizing the collective wisdom their team has to offer. They often empower employees to take some minor decisions and they like to breed them to be future leaders. In stressful or emergency situations, this style of leadership may not work as consensual decision-making can be too time-consuming. It is also known as a facilitative or participative leadership style.

4. Delegative: It is a style where leaders delegate tasks to their employees with fewer directives on what they are supposed to do and what not. It is also known as the laissez-faire leadership style. The French term *laissez faire* means *let them do*. It is most commonly found in entrepreneurial startups, where the leader puts full trust in their team so that they may focus on executing the company's overall strategy. The advantage of this least intrusive style is that it can result in an empowered group of employees. But the disadvantage is that it can constrain their development. At times, they might need some mentoring, which they may not get from a laissez-faire leader.

5. Pacesetting: In this type of leadership, a leader leads by setting an example for the team to follow. Such a leader is very knowledgeable and looked upon as an expert in his/her discipline. This type of leadership works in the case of a team with self-motivated high performers, who value continuous improvement and thrive under the direction of a pacesetting leader. However, the downside is that it can create a situation where team members feel they are being pushed too hard by a leader whose standards don't match with their own. Such a type of leadership is mostly found in startups.

6. Supportive: It is a style where leaders spend time identifying and nurturing the individual strengths of employees, bringing out the best in them, and helping them build behaviors to take action. It is similar to affiliate leadership, but more focus is on the individual growth of the employees. Pros of this style is that it facilitates a psychologically safe environment for the employees. Cons of this style is that sometimes employees might feel they are being micromanaged.

Imagine you are a manager of a private equity firm. You want to explore the impact of blockchain on your business. You have asked one of your senior direct reports to prepare a report with a business case. She has been a top performer for the last three years. She is excited about the task but does not know where to begin because she lacks experience and competence in blockchain:

If you are an autocratic leader, you will provide clear instructions on how the report and business case should look. You will provide her with a list of analyst reports and important documents on blockchain. You will ask her to enroll in specific online courses on blockchain. You will define a weekly plan and timeline for her. You will closely monitor her progress by scheduling weekly or even daily progress meetings.

If you are an affiliative leader, you will check with her how she feels doing this task or if she has any experience doing a similar task before. You could either provide her with materials on blockchain or ask her to do her own research. You could also suggest her an online course and do a constant follow-up on how she finds it. If she is uncomfortable or finds it difficult, you could suggest an alternative one. You could define a weekly plan and timeline but not be very rigid and demanding about her progress.

If you are a democratic leader, you will plan the structure of the report and business case together with her. You will also work together to search reports, documents, online courses, weekly plans, and timelines. You may not be equally or heavily involved with her in the task and will let her do a majority of the tasks. But the decision and agreements would be made collectively by you and her.

If you are a delegative leader, you will provide her with empowerment and autonomy to complete the task. You will not be involved in how she does it. What would matter to you is the result. You will expect her to drive this activity completely and take the initiative of scheduling weekly progress meetings. You will not be bothered much if she does not schedule a few of these. You will expect her to complete the task on her own and would prefer to offer the least support possible.

If you are a pacesetting leader, you would probably explain the purpose behind the task of delivering a report and a business case on blockchain. You would take the charge for first few days and set an example before her on how the task is supposed to be done. You would take the lead in finding material, registering her for courses, and preparing a weekly plan and timeline. Once you feel she can manage, you will let her drive on her own. You would like to have weekly updates on her progress.

If you are a supportive leader, you will empower her to complete the task on her own. You would expect her to find material, online courses and prepare a weekly plan and a timeline. But when she hits a roadblock and needs your help, you will proactively jump in to coach and support to resolve the issues or connect her with the right contacts. You would like to have weekly updates on her progress but would be flexible if she misses scheduling a few meetings.

Research has shown that there is no single best leadership style. When contemplating solutions to leadership challenges, it's important to be aware of the different strengths and weaknesses within these types of leadership styles. Often, you'll need a mix of two or more to achieve your goals. Sometimes, a teammate needs a hug. Other times, a teammate needs direction or constructive criticism. And sometimes, they need to be left alone to do their job. Choosing the right style to fit each situation is a key element of leadership effectiveness.

However, in the digital age, this may not be true. The delegative, supportive, and affiliative styles of leadership are more appreciated and encouraged. A survey was conducted by Digiculum, where 102 leaders belonging to different organizations across different industries across the globe were asked which leadership style they think is the best and would like to adopt more frequently for driving digital transformation.

Following was the outcome:

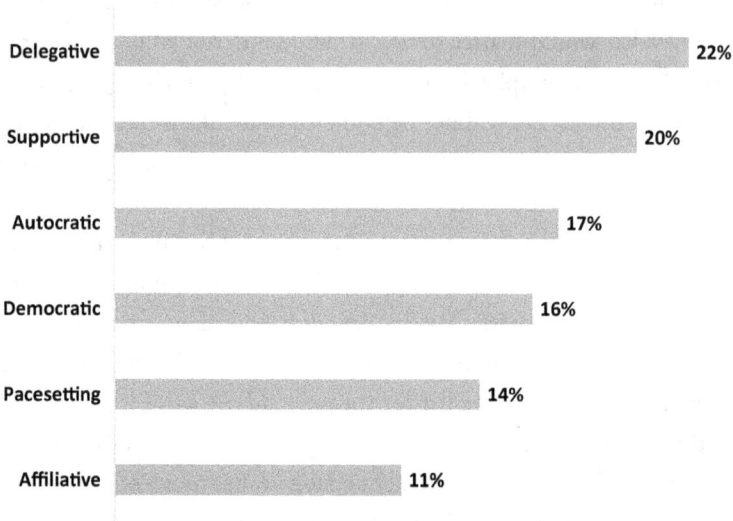

Figure 1.8 *Top leadership styles for driving digital transformation as per the leaders*

Another survey was conducted by Digiculum, where 235 employees from organizations across different industries across the globe were asked what type of leadership style they would prefer their leaders should adopt more frequently for driving digital transformation. Following was the outcome:

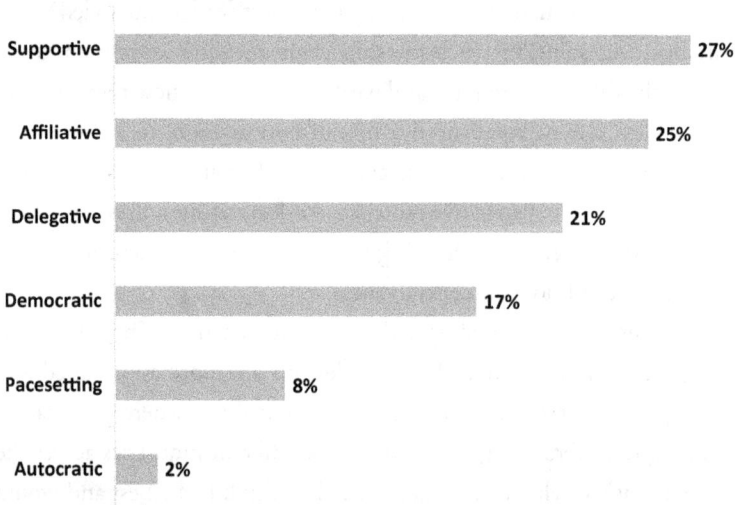

Figure 1.9 *Top leadership styles for driving digital transformation as per the employees*

Based on detailed interviews, a mapping of behaviors was done. Following were the observations:

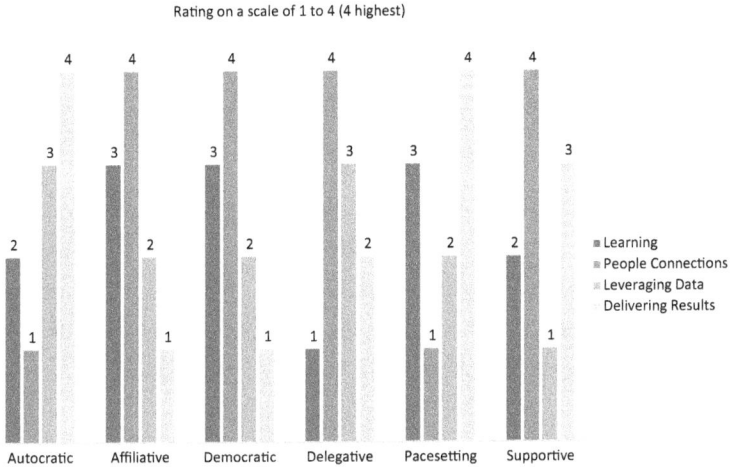

Figure 1.10 Leadership styles and behaviors mapping

For autocratic leadership style, the top behavior is delivering results, and the least behavior is people connections.

For affiliative leadership style, the top behavior is people connections, and the least behavior is delivering results.

For democratic leadership style, the top behavior is people connections, and the least behavior is delivering results.

For delegative leadership style, the top behavior is people connections, and the least behavior is learning.

For pacesetting leadership style, the top behavior is delivering results, and the least behavior is people connections.

For supportive leadership style, the top behavior is people connections, and the least behavior is leveraging data.

Leadership style	Top behavior	Least behavior
Autocratic	Delivering results	People connections
Affiliative	People connections	Delivering results
Democratic	People connections	Delivering results
Delegative	People connections	Learning
Pacesetting	Delivering results	People connections
Supportive	People connections	Leveraging data

Activating the Leadership Brand

Following are the two steps to activate your leadership brand:

1) Assessing your leadership style
2) Building your leadership brand.

Step 1: Assessing your leadership style

To determine your dominant leadership style, complete the following assessment containing six sections with 10 statements per section. Based on to what extent you agree or disagree, provide a score for each of them on a scale of 1 to 6, 1: strongly disagree, 2: disagree, 3: somewhat disagree, 4: somewhat agree, 5: agree, and 6: strongly agree. Calculate the total score for each section.

#	Statements	Scoring
	Section 1	
1	I always tell my subordinates/direct reports exactly what to do.	
2	I always speak my mind without considering much how other people feel.	
3	I am driven by a quest for unique achievements.	
4	I make quick decisions.	
5	I seldom involve my subordinates in decision-making.	
6	I execute my decisions fast.	
7	I am very result-oriented.	
8	I do not like it when my team disagrees with my views.	
9	I like to closely supervise my team.	
10	I seldom coach or mentor my team.	
	Total score	
	Section 2	
11	I connect very well with my team.	
12	I genuinely care about my team.	
13	I openly share my thoughts and feelings with my team and expect them to do the same.	
14	I always consider how my decision would make other people feel.	
15	My team feels very comfortable with me.	
16	I have a large and wide professional network.	
17	I do not like to micromanage my team.	
18	I am good at influencing people.	

#	Statements	Scoring
19	I am very receptive to change.	
20	I am open to new ideas and suggestions from my team.	
	Total score	
	Section 3	
21	I strongly believe in teamwork and collaboration.	
22	I seek my team's views and perspectives before making a decision.	
23	I am open to people challenging my views.	
24	I facilitate knowledge sharing with my team.	
25	I recognize people for their contributions.	
26	I offer feedback to people when they make mistakes.	
27	I give everyone in my team an opportunity to participate and speak during the meetings.	
28	I often keep people engaged at work.	
29	My team feels their voices and opinions are heard.	
30	My team often feels motivated at work.	
	Total score	
	Section 4	
31	I often delegate tasks to my team.	
32	I have a high trust and confidence in my team.	
33	I seldom follow up with my team after I delegate a task to them.	
34	I empower people.	
35	I seldom tell my team what to do.	
36	I believe that freedom and autonomy are the best team motivators.	
37	I am good at identifying my team's skills and talents.	
38	I seldom offer any feedback to my team.	
39	I strive to offer a good work–life balance to my team.	
40	I take full responsibility when my team makes a mistake in executing a task.	
	Total score	
	Section 5	
41	I exemplify good leadership.	
42	I set high standards of work.	
43	I set high expectations for my team.	
44	I often keep my team motivated.	
45	I have good knowledge and expertise in the area of my work.	
46	My team often seeks my advice and consultation when faced with issues.	

(Continued)

(*Continued*)

#	Statements	Scoring
47	I often do things quickly.	
48	I often do things accurately.	
49	I often accomplish my targets and goals.	
50	I provide constant feedback to my team.	
	Total score	
	Section 6	
51	I offer constant support to my team to complete a task.	
52	I am always available whenever my team needs me.	
53	I like to develop and coach people.	
54	I generally encourage the team to come up with their own solutions to problems.	
55	I believe more in execution than planning.	
56	I like to cultivate future leaders for my organization.	
57	I bring out the best in my team.	
58	I often share my knowledge and experience with my team.	
59	My team is seldom demotivated.	
60	I believe feedback is important for my team's development.	
	Total score	

Identify the section with the total highest and second-highest scores. They are your primary and secondary dominant leadership styles. Use the following legend:

Section 1: Autocratic
Section 2: Affiliative
Section 3: Democratic
Section 4: Delegative
Section 5: Pacesetting
Section 6: Supportive

Step 2: Building a leadership brand

The following are the three components of building a leadership brand:

1. Developing self-awareness
2. Assessing personal core values
3. Assessing changing organizational needs

Developing self-awareness

Self-awareness is the conscious knowledge of one's own character and feelings. It is of two types: internal self-awareness and external self-awareness. Internal self-awareness is about how clearly we see our values, passions, aspirations, strengths, and weaknesses fit with the environment. External self-awareness is about how people view us in terms of the preceding factors.

If we split each of the two types of self-awareness into high and low levels, we have *four self-awareness archetypes*, developed by Dr. Tasha Eurich, which can be plotted on a two-by-two matrix as shown in Figure 1.11.

Seekers: They don't yet know who they are, what they stand for, or how their team sees them. As a result, they might feel stuck and frustrated with their performance and relationships.

Pleasers: They can be so focused on appearing a certain way to others that they could be overlooking what matters to them. Over time, they tend to make choices that aren't in service of their own success and fulfillment.

Introspectors: They are clear on who they are but don't challenge their own views or search for blind spots by getting feedback from others. This can harm their relationships and limit their success.

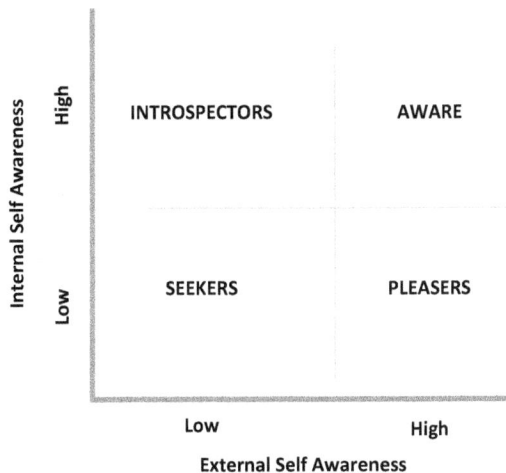

Figure 1.11 Self-awareness archetypes

Aware: They know who they are, what they want to accomplish, and seek out and value other's opinions. This is where leaders begin to fully realize the true benefits of self-awareness.

Self-awareness can be developed in the following three steps:

a. Reflect: Reflect on the attributes that you know about yourself.
b. Seek: Seek feedback from customers, peers, supervisors, and direct reports.
c. Conquer: Conquer your blind spots using the Johari window.

a. Reflect

Complete the following assessment containing 24 behavior statements. Based on to what extent you agree or disagree, provide a score for each of them on a scale of 1 to 5, 1: seldom, 2: rarely, 3: sometimes, 4: often, and 5: always.

#	Behavior statements	Score
1	I have a clear understanding of customer business.	
2	I can effectively translate customer needs into solutions.	
3	I can put into perspective how my work relates to customer success.	
4	I continuously seek feedback from customers to identify improvement.	
5	I establish clear, realistic timelines for goal accomplishment.	
6	I establish methods for monitoring and measuring progress.	
7	I track performance against customer requirements.	
8	I foster a sense of urgency in others to achieve goals.	
9	I facilitate the team activities effectively.	
10	I intervene appropriately to resolve conflict.	
11	I support useful changes and identify ways to improve the efficiency of future work.	
12	I work productively in the face of ambiguity or uncertainty.	
13	I demonstrate a good understanding of my organization's vision, mission, and strategy.	
14	I encourage others to look at problems and processes in new ways.	
15	I routinely try out new methods, processes, and technologies.	
16	I leverage ideas from others and evaluate them to ensure business viability.	
17	I make accurate evaluations of people's capabilities and fit.	

#	Behavior statements	Score
18	I share credit and give visibility to others.	
19	I relate well to a variety of people regardless of their level or background.	
20	I stand behind the decisions of the organization, superiors, or team.	
21	I share information and viewpoints openly and directly with others.	
22	I demonstrate an interest in people and their growth and development.	
23	I apply and seek out the knowledge and expertise of others.	
24	I adopt best practices and lessons learned from within and outside the organization.	

b. Seek

Send the following assessment to your peers, supervisors, direct reports, stakeholders, and even customers, if possible. Ask them to complete the following assessment containing 24 statements. Based on to what extent they agree or disagree with the statement about, provide a score for each of them on a scale of 1 to 5, 1: seldom, 2: rarely, 3: sometimes, 4: often, 5: always.

If others don't know or have not observed a certain trait or attribute about you, they must write *not observed.*

#	Behavior statements	Score
1	Demonstrates a clear understanding of customer business.	
2	Can effectively translate customer needs into solutions.	
3	Has a good understanding of how work relates to customer success.	
4	Continuously seeks feedback from customers to identify improvement.	
5	Establishes clear, realistic timelines for goal accomplishment.	
6	Establishes methods for monitoring and measuring progress.	
7	Tracks performance against customer requirements.	
8	Fosters a sense of urgency in others to achieve goals.	
9	Facilitates team activities effectively.	
10	Resolves conflicts within the team.	
11	Supports useful changes and identifies ways to improve the efficiency of future work.	
12	Works productively in the face of ambiguity or uncertainty.	
13	Demonstrates a good understanding of the organization's vision, mission, and strategy.	

(*Continued*)

(*Continued*)

#	Behavior statements	Score
14	Encourages others to look at problems and processes in new ways.	
15	Tries out new methods, processes, and technologies.	
16	Seeks ideas from others and evaluates them to ensure business viability.	
17	Makes accurate evaluations of people's capabilities and fit.	
18	Shares credit and gives visibility to others.	
19	Relates well to a variety of people regardless of their level or background.	
20	Supports the decisions of the organization, superiors, or team.	
21	Shares information and viewpoints openly and directly with others.	
22	Demonstrates an interest in people and their growth and development.	
23	Leverages the knowledge and expertise of others.	
24	Adopts best practices and lessons learned from within and outside the organization.	

Compare the scores using the following score difference sheet:

Behaviors	Reflect score	Seek score	Score difference
1			
2			
3			
4			
...			
24			

If the seek score is *not observed*, then write NA in the score difference.

c. Conquer

A Johari window model is shown in Figure 1.12. It was created by psychologists Joseph Luft and Harrington Ingham in 1955, and is used primarily in self-help groups and corporate settings as a heuristic exercise.[20] Luft and Ingham named their model *Johari* using a combination of their first names.

Based on the matrix, there are four quadrants:

	Known to Self	Unknown to Self
Known to Others	**ARENA** *Public Self*	**BLIND SPOTS** *Blind Self*
Unknown to Others	**MASK** *Private Self*	**UNCONSCIOUS** *Unknown Self*

Figure 1.12 Johari window

Mask: Known to self and unknown to others. It is your private self.

Arena: Known to self and known to others. It is your public self.

Blind spots: What others know about you, but you don't see. It is your blind self.

Unconscious: Neither you know, nor others know. It is your unknown self.

Use the following sheet and categorize each of the 24 behavior statements in the assessment under the appropriate square:

Arena	Blind spots
- - - - --	- - - - --
Mask	**Unconscious**
- - - - --	Exclude this section in the analysis

Compare the score difference for each behavior using the score difference sheet:

- If the score difference is 1 or less, move it under Arena.
- If the score difference is more than 1, move it under Blind spots.
- If the score difference is NA, move it under Mask.

Blind spots are the ones that others see about you, but you don't see. Make a note of them and reflect on how you can overcome. You may reach out directly to the people who see them in you if you need more clarification.

2. Assessing personal core values

In his book *The Compound Effect*, author Darren Hardy has offered a framework for assessing your personal values. He says, "Your values are your GPS navigation system for life. Getting them defined and properly calibrated is one of the most important steps in redirecting your life toward your grandest vision."

Assessment

Answer the following questions thoughtfully:

1. Who is the person I respect most in life? What are their core values?	2. Who is my best friend, and what are his/her top three qualities?
3. If I could have more of any one quality instantly, what would it be?	4. What are three things I hate (e.g., cruelty to animals, credit card companies, deforestation)?
5. Which three people in the world do I dislike the most, and why?	6. Which personality trait, attribute, or quality do people compliment me with the most?
7. What are the three most important values I want to pass on to my children?	8. If I were to teach a graduating high-school class values that would give them the best opportunity for success in life, what would those be, and why?
9. If I had enough money to retire tomorrow, what values would I continue to hold?	10. What values do I see being valid 100 years from now?

Now look at your answers. Do you notice any reoccurring themes? Considering what you've observed in others, what others have observed about you, what you want from others, and things you would fight for or against, create a list of your top 10 values or even fewer (in any order) in the following:

#	Top values
1	
2	
3	
4	
5	
6	
7	
8	
9	
10	

You must shortlist six. Put x next to the values you're sure about. Then take the ones you feel are important but aren't sure if they are top-six material, and put them in pairs. Think about two of those values side by side and ask yourself which of the two is more important, eliminating the other. Keep pitting the survivors against each other until you're down to six. If some of the values you listed are just two words describing the same idea, combine them.

List your top six values in the following table prioritized in order of importance.

#	Top values
1	
2	
3	
4	
5	
6	

Consider two values at a time and try to choose which would you fight for, or even die defending. Select the top three values.

My top three values in life are as follows:

1. _____

2. _____

3. _____

3. Assessing changing organizational needs

To understand the organization's needs, consider the following questions:

1. What are the key strengths of my organization?	2. What are the top challenges and pain points for my organization?
3. What are the new business opportunities for my organization?	4. What are the threats to our business?
5. How is my organization better than my competitors?	6. How are my competitors better than my organization?
7. What are the things that customers like about my business?	8. What are the things that customers dislike about my business?
9. What are the things that employees like working in my organization?	10. What are the things that employees dislike working in my organization?
11. Is the company's value proposition well understood by the employees?	12. Is the company's value proposition well understood by the customers?
13. Does the company have a clear and concrete strategy?	14. Do the employees understand and relate to the strategy?

Now, take a look at your answers. Are you able to identify some reoccurring needs? Make a list of the top 10 or fewer needs (in any order) in the following table:

#	Top needs
1	
2	
3	
4	
5	
6	
7	
8	

#	Top needs
9	
10	

You must shortlist six. Put *x* next to the needs that you are sure about. Then take the ones you feel are important but aren't sure if they are top-six needs and put them in pairs. Think about two of those needs side by side and ask yourself which of the two is more important, eliminating the other. Keep pitting the survivors against each other until you're down to six. If some of the needs you listed are just two words describing the same idea, combine them.

List your top six needs in the following table:

#	Top needs
1	
2	
3	
4	
5	
6	

Consider two needs at a time and try to choose the most urgent and important for your business having a huge impact on it. Select the top three needs.

The top three organizational needs are as follows:

1. _____
2. _____
3. _____

Leadership brand statement

Based on observations and data collected from the preceding three assessments, write a new leadership brand statement. You can use the following template:

I am a _____(your style)_____digital leader believing in _____(why) aspiring to do _____(what)_____ by _____(how)_____

You can also consider the following questions while preparing your brand statement:

- *Why* do I want to be a digital leader? What do I believe in?
- *What* actions do I need to take?
- *How* can I realize my beliefs?

For example:

I am a democratic digital leader believing in making an impact on different industries and societies by implementing digital transformation through trust, empathy, and hard work.

Summary

- Digital leadership is the set of behaviors a leader must demonstrate in the digital age.
- The main driver behind digital leadership is digital transformation.
- The four essential behaviors of a digital leader are learning new skills, connecting with people, leveraging data, and delivering results.
- The four key competencies of a digital leader are growth mindset, empathy, informed decision-making, and fast execution.
- Growth mindset is a frame of mind where people believe that their skills are not inbuilt but can be developed through efforts and dedication.
- Empathy is the ability to understand other people's emotions. It is about understanding what others think, feel, and will (desire).
- Informed decision-making involves making decisions based on accurate, reliable, and relevant information. It involves gathering and analyzing data, considering multiple perspectives, and using critical thinking skills to evaluate options and make the best choice.

- Fast execution is the ability of a leader to take rapid actions in both certain and uncertain environments.
- The six popular widely accepted leadership styles are autocratic, affiliative, democratic, delegative, pacesetting, and supportive.
- The three components of building a leadership brand are
  - Developing self-awareness
  - Assessing personal core values
  - Assessing changing organizational needs

CHAPTER 2

Competency 1: Growth Mindset

At a corporate networking event, I met with an ex-colleague of mine, let us call her Vrinda, who is currently the vice president of sales at one of the leading telecommunications companies. It was interesting to listen to her presentation on selling a real-time data analytics product based on AI and Amazon Web Services (AWS) cloud to her client. It was the first big sale for her company since they had invested in cloud, data analytics, and AI, three years ago. They had introduced intensive upskilling and reskilling programs for their employees on these digital technologies. At the end of the presentation, when I met her in person, I wanted to clarify some of the points she touched upon very briefly in her presentation and did not go into details. I asked, "Did you use Amazon Kinesis service for real-time data analytics or was it from some other third-party vendor?"

She replied, "I don't know."

"Did you use any of AWS AI services in your product?" I asked.

She again replied, "I don't know."

After a pause, I asked, "Is AWS your sole cloud service provider for developing your products? Or do you also develop in-house using the private cloud?"

To this, she replied, "I am not so sure. I need to check with my team."

I saw her getting uncomfortable with the high-level technical questions. To make her feel comfortable, I eased the conversation a bit. I asked her about the learning programs on data analytics in her company. To which she replied that they have a partnership with a vendor that offers certification programs for the employees. Many have enrolled in them and the response is quite good.

I asked her, "Have you enrolled in any of these certifications?"

She replied:

Yes. I started with the basic data analytics course a month ago. I watched some self-learning videos. But then things started getting too technical. It was difficult for me to understand since I don't come from a technical background. Also, it was too difficult to manage it along with my daily job. I put it on hold for the moment.

Five months later, I met her at the Stockholm-Arlanda airport. We both were traveling on the same flight to London on a business trip. I asked her, "How is your data analytics certification coming along?"

"Still the same. No progress since we met last. I don't think I would be able to do it. You know, I don't have a technical background." We changed the topic and began conversing on other things.

I understand that technical skills were not required in her job. But when working for a technical company and selling data analytics products with AWS solutions, it's always better to have a very basic high-level know-how of the technology. The issue with most leaders today is that they are somewhat reluctant when it comes to learning. Some say that they don't have time for learning. Some say that they don't need them in their daily jobs. Some start learning, but they encounter challenges and difficulties in the middle of the course. So, they give up. Leaders do not need to have deep technical knowledge about digital transformation technologies. They can always refer to the technical subject matter experts for advice. But at least, they need to know an overview of them explaining what impact they have on business. Leaders are supposed to be the champions and advocates of a learning culture in their firms. Imagine how ironic it sounds when they themselves don't learn. Wouldn't Vrinda have been more comfortable in answering my question on Amazon kinesis I asked her at the event, if she had completed the certification? Her gradual buildup of technical knowledge would have increased her confidence, enabling her to learn more. It would have made her more proactive and confident at the customer or internal team meetings, discussing technical topics. Also, as a leader enabling digital transformation, it would have helped her set a good example before other employees in her firm.

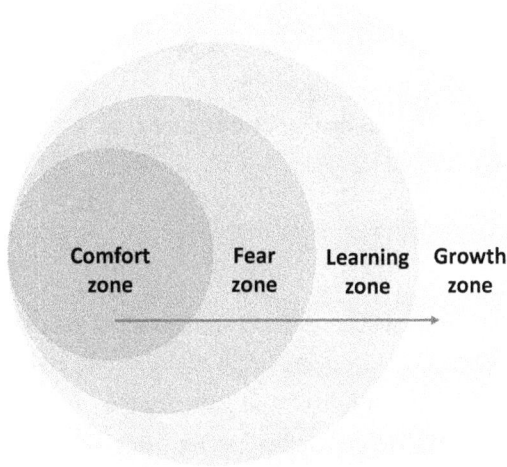

Figure 2.1 The four zones

To explain the psychology of a learner, the psychologists explain the following four zones: comfort, fear, learning, and growth.

In the *comfort* zone, you feel safe and in control. To learn a new skill, you need to step out of your comfort zone and enter the fear zone, which requires courage and determination. In the *fear* zone, there is no initial self-confidence. You find excuses to learn and are affected by other's opinions. Then, once you start learning, you overcome your fears and enter the *learning* zone, where you start acquiring new skills and deal with new challenges and problems. Then, gradually you become confident, safe, and in control. In other words, you start creating a new comfort zone. Once you develop sufficient proficiency for the new skill, you enter the *growth* zone, where you realize your goals and objectives and start growing in your career.[1]

But why are people not willing to step out of their comfort zones? Why are they reluctant to learn? It is because of their *fixed* mindsets. Research on mindsets has been conducted by Carol Dweck, a psychology professor at Stanford University.

She says:

For decades I have been studying why some people succeed while people, who are equally talented, do not. And over the years I have discovered that people's MINDSETS play a crucial role in this process.

In her book *Mindsets: The New Psychology of Success*, Prof. Carol Dweck explains that there are two types of mindsets: *fixed* mindset and *growth* mindset. These two mindsets have a major impact on how we learn and achieve our goals. The two characteristics that differentiate them are as follows:

- Belief
- Focus

The preceding two characteristics give rise to certain behaviors, which are considered as the by-products of characteristics.[2] Figure 2.2 shows characteristics of people with fixed and growth mindset and their respective behaviors related to effort, challenges, feedback, mistakes, and other's success.

People with a fixed mindset believe that skills are born. Either someone has them or does not have them. People with a growth mindset believe that skills are built. One can learn any skill through continuous practice and dedication.

People with a fixed mindset focus on the outcomes. They are keener on how they would look and what would other people think about them if they failed to achieve a result. Whereas people with a growth mindset

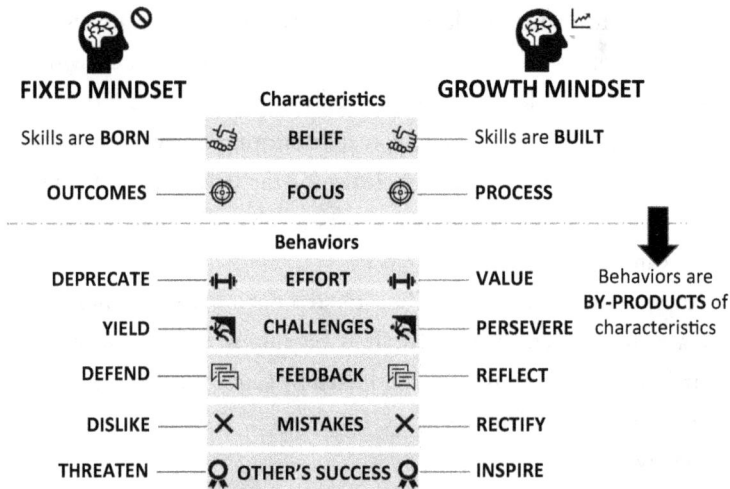

Figure 2.2 Characteristics and behaviors

Source: Illustrated by Amit Prabhu.

are more focused on the process of learning than the result. They enjoy the journey and persevere through it, no matter how hard the process is. They take the challenges as learning opportunities.

People with a fixed mindset deprecate the efforts, whereas those with a growth mindset value the efforts. Learning requires effort. There is no substitute for hard work. Efforts require one to step out of one's comfort zone to learn new things. Those with fixed mindsets have a focus on the end results, and they want to see them fast, and they want them now. If they don't see an immediate improvement, they begin doubting the efforts and become demotivated to put more consistently. Those with a growth mindset are able to see the link between the efforts and the mastery of skill—the end result. They believe that consistent efforts will pay off eventually even if they don't see immediate tangible results. It does not mean that people with fixed mindsets are not hard-working and do not put in effort. They have worked hard to develop the skills needed to excel at their jobs. However, when it comes to learning a new skill, they don't appreciate the efforts required as they are unwilling to move out of their comfort zone.

People with a fixed mindset yield to the challenges, whereas those with a growth mindset persevere through them. Learning a new skill comes with lots of challenges. Sometimes, learning a topic appears much easier. Based on that, one makes an estimation of the time and effort required. When one starts to learn, one becomes aware of the hidden challenges. The estimation of time and effort required goes wrong. When more time and effort are needed, those with fixed mindsets find it very difficult to make these new adjustments. When things become too stressful and overwhelming, they give up. Those with a growth mindset are able to adjust to the new settings. They sail through the challenges smoothly.

People with a fixed mindset defend when given feedback, whereas those with a growth mindset reflect on feedback. Feedback on learning can be both positive and negative, which normally points out the areas where one can do better and suggest a plan of action to improve further. The first reaction of those with a fixed mindset on receiving feedback is that they become defensive. It is because of the efforts required to execute the plan of action. Those with a growth mindset reflect on the feedback they receive. They are prepared to put more effort into the plan of action.

Everyone makes mistakes while learning. People with a fixed mindset dislike it when their mistakes are pointed out either privately or publicly. With the latter, the effect can be more severe. They spend some time arguing or justifying how right they are or what are their intentions behind them. This is mostly observed with an expert in a certain field with a fixed mindset who is learning a new skill. However, those with a growth mindset accept their mistakes both privately and publicly and take immediate steps to rectify them.

People with a fixed mindset view other people's success as a threat. Whereas those with a growth mindset are inspired by other people's success. In most cases, people desire to learn a new skill. But they are too complacent to take the necessary actions needed to get there. There is a difference between desiring to learn and learning. But when your close colleagues successfully learn a skill, those with a fixed mindset feel threatened. They consider it as a risk to their current jobs. They change their approach and behavior toward them. Whereas a person with a growth mindset would get motivated by them. If he or she can do it, I can do it too. They develop more respect toward their colleagues and approach them to learn from their inspiring success stories.

A growth mindset is important for a digital leader because:

- It motivates one to learn new things.
- It builds resilience in a learner.
- It sustains hunger for learning.

Ronald von Bruch (name changed) was the head of partnerships at a global multinational retail company based in Nordics. He was responsible for building new partnerships and maintaining the existing ones with external suppliers. He had a nontechnical background and had been in this position for the past four years. His company was planning to sign a contract worth millions of euros with one of the leading public cloud service providers (CSP). It was about migrating several IT applications and large amount of data onto the cloud using different services offered by the CSP. The following week, Ronald had a meeting with the head of sales, sales managers, and a few technical experts from the CSP. He had invited two people from his team, and from the IT team he had invited one cloud expert and one solution architect, to accompany him to the meeting. The CSP team began delivering the presentation that included details about their company, cloud products and services, and their success stories with other clients. It was a very interactive and engaging team meeting. There were lots of discussions and questions back and forth. Ronald was impressed by the new opportunities cloud would bring to its company. At the same time, he was feeling a bit demotivated as he couldn't engage much in the discussion due to his lack of knowledge on cloud. It was when he decided that he would build his knowledge on cloud, at least up to the level where he could have meaningful and engaging discussions with others.

Ronald demonstrated a growth mindset. He was *motivated*. He believed that he could build the necessary skills and knowledge outside the area of his expertise. He began with some YouTube videos on cloud. He could not follow much. Then he signed up for a beginner's course on cloud on his company's learning platform. The first two videos were good. But then things started becoming too technical. The more he tried to grasp, the more confused and frustrated he became. But Ronald was *resilient*.

One of his colleagues recommended my course on Udemy: *Business Impact of Digital Transformation Technologies*. It is a pure beginner's course developed for people with both technical and nontechnical backgrounds. He enrolled for the course online and liked the content very much. He wrote me a private message if I could have a one-on-one paid training with him on cloud, either online or in person. Teaching being my passion, I immediately replied to him with a *yes*. We agreed to meet in the evenings online for an hour, three times a week.

During our first meeting, I inquired about his motivation behind learning cloud. After hearing his story, I became quite impressed. It takes courage for someone to step out of one's comfort zone at a senior management level, late in one's career, to explore a new domain one has never been in before. I had just finished reading the book *Mindsets: The New Psychology of Success* by Carol Dweck, and I saw a good example in front of me. I suggested him to aim for the basic-level certification of the CSP with whom his company was planning to partner. The knowledge of cloud is very vast and exhaustive. It could be very overwhelming at times. Preparation for the certification exam streamlines one's efforts and provides one with some focus and direction. Also, it provides one with confidence and credibility, and can open a new career door altogether. Ronald agreed.

I started teaching him the basics of cloud and its impact on the business, with the aim of completing the certification in the next six months. The learning curve was not easy. There were challenges. The biggest one was to take off time from his very busy schedule. But Ronald was determined. He started to enjoy the journey of learning. He was never afraid to ask apparently the silliest or obvious question, and he took the feedback I gave him very constructively. Every day he started becoming better and better at his knowledge on cloud.

Finally, it was time for the certification exam. Ronald failed on his first attempt. But that never made him feel unworthy or developed any kind of setback in him. In fact, he boldly announced to everyone at his team meeting about his failure and his hope of clearing the certification on his second attempt. After three weeks, he appeared once again for the certification exam. And this time, he cleared it. I was the first person to whom he broke the news over the phone. Ronald was overjoyed. A few days later, we met over lunch and celebrated his success.

But this didn't stop him from learning. He was *hungry* to learn more. He also appeared for certification exams from the other two largest global CSPs. He cleared them both on the first attempt. He was now more confident and comfortable engaging in conversations on the cloud. He was an inspiration for his team, most of them with nontechnical backgrounds, and also for other leaders in his company.

> Had Ronald had a fixed mindset, he would not have believed that he could ever develop cloud skills and probably would have never stepped out of his comfort zone.
>
> Had Ronald had a fixed mindset, he would have constantly worried about how he would feel and what others would say to him if he failed the certification exam.
>
> Had Ronald had a fixed mindset, he would have not valued the efforts he was putting day in and day out and would have considered it to be a waste of time.

Had Ronald had a fixed mindset, he would have succumbed to the learning challenges and would have given up.

Had Ronald had a fixed mindset, he would have felt envious if some other leader in his organization had acquired this certification and felt threatened.

But he had a growth mindset. That's why, he could learn despite all odds.

After two quarters, there was a reorganization in the company and a new position—head of cloud services—was opened. Ronald applied for it and he was selected because of his decade of leadership experience with the company and his knowledge on cloud. Currently, Ronald is a champion of cloud and AI learning programs in his firm, inspiring most people with nontechnical backgrounds to learn. He wants to learn and grow more.

Carol Dweck further explains that these mindsets are not permanent. They are not two different individuals—one with a fixed and other with a growth mindset. At different times, on different days, and in different situations, one can be in a fixed mindset or a growth mindset. Figure 2.3 shows a mindset spectrum. You lie at a certain point on the spectrum depending on the circumstances.

Your characteristics determine your mindset—either fixed or growth, which then impacts your behaviors, which determine your growth, as shown in Figure 2.4.

A growth mindset can be implemented at an individual and at an organizational level. A digital leader must make sure that he/she cultivates a growth

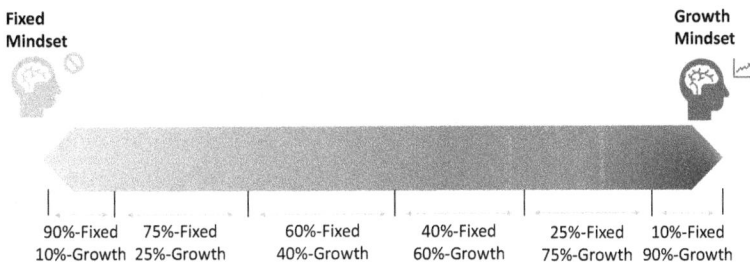

Figure 2.3 Mindset spectrum

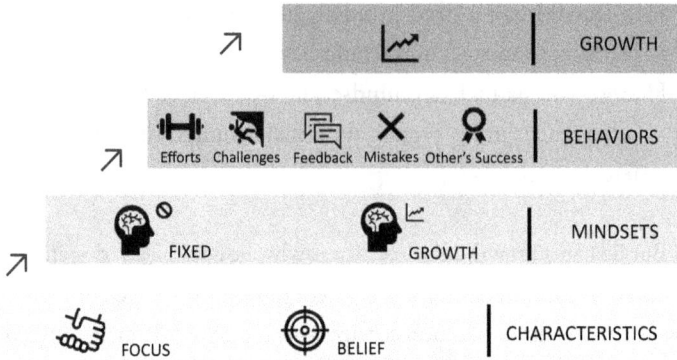

Figure 2.4 Characteristics impact your growth

mindset first and then cultivates it for the team. Two examples of growth mindset implementation at the organizational level are Telenor and Microsoft.

Telenor, a 160-year-old Norwegian multinational telecommunications company headquartered near Oslo, serving 172 million customers across Scandinavia and Asia, underwent a technological change. To stay successful in a highly competitive and fast-changing business landscape, Telenor's leadership development team decided to introduce a growth mindset culture. A group of Telenor's senior managers were the first ones to go through the growth mindset training program. After positive feedback from the one-day workshop (which was part of a four-day executive leadership development program) with the 60 leaders, the rollout for the company's 22,000 employees began. It included revamping the company's performance management process and innovations. Positive reinforcements and role modeling efforts continued to help embed growth mindset behaviors so that they could become habits. For example, the CEO and CHRO made sure to use growth mindset terminology in monthly townhall, and office workers used growth mindset-related terms in meetings and conversations. Some leaders sat at different desks every day to interact with new colleagues; and managers had developmental conversations with direct reports. On the Telenor campus learning platform, employees could earn a growth mindset learning badge and free access to further learning modules or programs as a reward for completing various levels of online self-study. In addition to learning and habit-formation efforts, Telenor was also embedding a growth mindset into team development initiatives, executive leadership programs, talent reviews, and high-potential assessments. In terms of innovation, the term *working red* was invented, symbolizing the new ways of failing fast and learning from it, rapid prototyping, and focusing on learning rather than just achieving end results.[3]

Before Satya Nadella took charge as the third CEO of Microsoft on February 4, 2014, the culture at the company was not conducive to learning and innovation. Microsoft was very much focused on realizing Bill Gates's vision to put a PC on every office desk and in every home driven by the windows operating system and MS office software, its two major and dominant cash cows. Employees who suggested any alternate innovations were accused of deviation from Microsoft's Windows strategy. The work culture at Microsoft was rigid. Each employee had to prove to everyone that he or she was the smartest person in the room. Delivering on time and meeting the numbers was everything that mattered. It cared less about how people feel working in the company. Meetings were very formal, and the organizational structure was hierarchical. If a senior leader wanted to seek feedback from some junior employee, he or she needed to invite that person's managers. Microsoft had a stack ranking performance management system, where employees were given the rating as top, good, average, below average, and poor, using a forced distribution. It meant that 10 percent of the people would always receive a poor rating, regardless of how much they contributed. Such a system paralyzed collaboration and knowledge sharing between the employees as they feared that giving away their best ideas would damage their position. Many of their top talents left the company and joined Google, who were paying employees 23 percent above the industry average. Microsoft's stock price was stalled, even though revenue had tripled, and profits had doubled during Ballmer's tenure as CEO from 2000 to 2014. An industry analyst Jan Dawson summarized:[4]

It was an enormously profitable company. They were in no danger of going out of business soon—it was just a question of whether they would go into a permanent decline.

On the first day when Satya took charge as the new CEO, he wrote a letter to all the employees. Following are some of the key excerpts from it:[5]

> Today is a very humbling day for me. It reminds me of my very first day at Microsoft, 22 years ago. Like you, I had a choice about where to come to work. I came here because I believed Microsoft was the best company in the world. I saw then how clearly, we empower people to do magical things with our creations and ultimately make the world a better place. I knew there was no better company to join if I wanted to make a difference. This is the very same inspiration that continues to drive me today.
>
> I truly believe that each of us must find meaning in our work. The best work happens when you know that it's not just work, but something that will improve other people's lives. This is the opportunity that drives each of us at this company.
>
> Many companies aspire to change the world. But very few have all the elements required: talent, resources, and perseverance. Microsoft has proven that it has all three in abundance. And as the new CEO, I can't ask for a better foundation.
>
> Let's build on this foundation together.

In this letter, Satya demonstrated *belief,* the important characteristic of a growth mindset.

In early 2015, Satya's wife Anu gave him a best-selling book by Carol Dweck *Mindsets: The New Psychology of Success.* She thought it could help him with some ideas for Microsoft. Satya became inspired by the book and decided to build a culture of learning based on a growth mindset on the belief that everyone can grow and develop; the potential is nurtured, not predetermined; and anyone can change their mindset. It was a shift from *know-it-alls* to *learn-it-alls.* Satya entrusted Kathleen Hogan, the chief people officer at Microsoft, an ex-McKinsey, to drive the cultural transformation based on a growth mindset. At an offsite meeting with 180 executives divided into 17 teams, they had an open dialogue on what kind of culture they wanted to have. After intense discussions and consultations with experts like Carol Dweck, three learning cultural pillars of growth mindset were articulated:

- Customer obsession
  An insatiable desire to learn about the customer needs from the outside world and bring that learning into Microsoft.
- Diversity and inclusion
  Make it possible for everyone to speak up so that everyone's ideas can come through. Inclusiveness would help us become open to learning about our own biases and changing our behaviors so that we can tap into the collective power of everyone at the company.
- One Microsoft
  We are one company, one Microsoft—not a confederation of fiefdoms. Innovation and competition don't respect our silos, so we have to learn to transcend those barriers.[6]

At Microsoft's global sales conference in Orlando in July 2015, Satya revealed a fresh company mission based on a growth mindset culture:

To empower every person and every organization on the planet to achieve more.

Through 2015 and 2016, Satya spoke widely about the importance of a growth mindset, thereby setting the tone for the culture. There were many changes made in the company, both big and small, that facilitated a culture of change. The infamous stack-ranking performance system was abolished and replaced by a continuous feedback and coaching system. The compensation process was redefined. Instead of basing rewards such as bonuses on an algorithm driven by employee ratings, managers were given a budget for compensation that they could hand out to deserving performers. Microsoft introduced its annual Hackathon *OneWeek*. It exemplified the new *one company* ethos. Employees were invited to step away from their work and work on a hack—a problem, that when solved, could benefit people, businesses, society, and the environment.[7]

Through his behavior, Satya demonstrated the characteristics of a growth mindset. Once he was invited as the keynote speaker at the Grace Hopper Celebration of Women in Computing, an annual event for women in the tech industry. During the Q&A, he was asked what advice he had for women seeking a pay raise who are not comfortable asking. He advised patience and knowing and having faith in the system will give you the raises as you go along. His comments went viral, provoking outrage. He was deemed ignorant of well-documented gender pay gaps. His commitment to diversity and inclusion was questioned. But Satya, rather than defending this mistake, completely owned it. In his e-mail to the employees, he said that he had answered the question completely wrong. It made a positive impression on his leadership team who became more committed to him. He came out to the entire company and said, "We are going to learn, and we are going to get a lot smarter."[8]

Today, Microsoft is again a magnet for top engineering talent, rated as one of the five best AI companies for employees. Satya has a Glassdoor employee approval of 95 percent. Satya said:

Our industry doesn't respect tradition. It respects innovation.

Microsoft has made some bold tech decisions such as investments in quantum computing, metaverse, and HoloLens, a holographic computer that enables people to interact with holograms. Today, over 95 percent of the Fortune 500 companies choose Azure, Microsoft's cloud computing service. It has built products and applications on Linux, an open-source software, Windows' bitter rival a decade ago. It established a partnership with LinkedIn, combining its 500 million professional users with the 85 million people who use Office 365, giving Microsoft a data source for its AI operations.[9]

The results of the implementation of a growth mindset at Microsoft were amazing. Employees were inspired to learn more. Knowledge-sharing sessions were on the rise. Different groups across the company were collaborating more. The employee satisfaction index was improved.

They felt the company was heading in the right direction and making the right choices for long-term success.[10]

Cultivating a Growth Mindset

The following framework would help one develop a growth mindset:

Step 1: Assessing your growth mindset

Step 2: Building a growth mindset

Step 1: Assessing your growth mindset

The following assessment contains 20 statements. Based on how closely you agree with the statements, give a rating on a scale of 1 to 6, 6: strongly agree, 5: agree, 4: somewhat agree, 3: somewhat disagree, 2: disagree, and 1: strongly disagree.

#	Statements	Rating
1	I can take up any role at my firm.	
2	I always make time from my daily routine to learn new skills and concepts.	
3	Talent is not natural; it needs to be developed.	
4	It is ok to make mistakes.	
5	I learn best only when I make mistakes.	
6	Hard work eventually pays off.	
7	Every day I get better and better at my work.	
8	I take efforts to develop people.	
9	I don't get frustrated when things don't happen my way.	
10	Better spend time on a difficult problem than skip it.	
11	In case of a failed decision, I don't blame others.	
12	I don't get annoyed when people give me negative feedback.	
13	I overcome my weaknesses.	
14	I don't get upset when corrected by my juniors.	
15	I don't feel envious when my coworkers get promoted.	
16	I don't feel threatened by my peers.	
17	I often share credit with others for success.	
18	Failures don't make me upset.	
19	I don't feel more stressed in uncertain situations.	
20	How things are done matters to me more than what needs to be done.	
	Average score	

Use the following table to map your growth mindset level:

Score range	Level
Average score > 5	Very high growth mindset
4 < Average score ≤ 5	High growth mindset
3 < Average score ≤ 4	Medium growth mindset
2 < Average score ≤ 3	Low growth mindset
1 < Average score ≤ 2	Very low growth mindset
Average score < 1	Negligible

Step 2: Building a growth mindset

There are three simple steps on how to build a growth mindset:

- Belief
- Action
- Focus

Belief helps to establish a purpose.
Action enables one to step out of comfort zone.
Focus helps to monitor progress.

Belief

Think of new skill/skills you would like to develop or any topic you would like to learn.

Answer the following questions:

- Why do you want to do it?
- What is the benefit of doing it?
- What is the disadvantage of not doing it?
- How strongly you believe you can do it? Rate your belief on a scale of 1 to 10 (1: lowest, 10: highest)

Fill in the following sheet:

New skills/learning topics	Belief rating
1.	
2.	
3.	
4.	
n.	

Actions

Once you make a list of new skills to learn and rate your beliefs, the next step is to identify the actions you need to take.

Answer the following questions:

- What specific actions will you take?
- What challenges are you likely to face?
- How strong is your commitment level to taking action? Rate on a scale of 1 to 10 (1: lowest, 10: highest)

Fill in the following sheet:

New skills/ learning topics	Belief rating	Actions to be taken	Commitment rating
1.			
2.			
3.			
4.			
n.			

Focus

Make sure you take action as per the plan. Instead of focusing on the result, focus on the continuous and daily progress.

Answer the following questions:

- How would you monitor your progress?
- What specific KPIs would you like to introduce?

New skills/ learning topics	Belief rating	Actions to be taken	Commitment rating	KPIs
1.				
2.				
3.				
4.				
n.				

Summary

- Fixed and growth mindsets have a major impact on how we learn and achieve our goals.
- Belief and focus are the two characteristics that differentiate them.
- A growth mindset is important for a digital leader because:
  o It motivates one to learn new things.
  o It builds resilience in a learner.
  o It sustains hunger for learning.
- At different times, on different days, in different situations, one can be in a fixed mindset or a growth mindset.
- Your characteristics determine your mindset—either fixed or growth, which then impacts your behaviors, which determines your growth.
- Growth mindset can be implemented at an individual level and at an organizational level.
- The three simple steps to build a growth mindset:
  o Belief
  o Action
  o Focus

CHAPTER 3

Competency 2: Empathy

Goran Bloch (name changed) had a good track record of working for a leading European IT and telecommunications company for over a decade. He had expertise in different telecom domains such as radio access network (RAN), core network, and business support systems (BSS). The air interface between the antenna (base station) and the wireless device is managed by RAN. A large network of such base stations is managed by the core network. BSS manage services such as user provisioning, billing, creating new voice and data plans, discounts, promotional offers, and so on. Recently, Goran developed an interest in data, AI, and cloud and wanted to work on such projects for telco customers. He took several online courses on data, AI, and generative AI to strengthen his knowledge on these technologies. He began preparing for certifications for popular public cloud providers such as AWS, Azure, and Google Cloud, also known as hyperscalers. He cleared all the certifications. As cloud, data, and AI were not the core competencies of Goran's current company, he struggled to find a new role internally. So, he decided to look for opportunities outside.

Seeing his telco background, knowledge, and cloud certifications on his LinkedIn profile, HR from a leading global IT consulting firm contacted him and asked if he would be interested in a role very closely matching his skills, they were looking to fill in. Goran cleared the first interview round with HR. He then had three rounds of interviews: one with the telco cloud project manager, one with the head of communications practice, and the final one with a senior colleague in the team. The scope of telco cloud project was to build a hybrid cloud infrastructure for the client and integrate data, AI, and genAI capabilities. It was just the kind of project Goran was passionate about and desperately wanted to work as his next career progression move. All the interviewers liked his background and experience and decided to offer him the position of consulting manager. But Goran wanted the position of senior consulting manager. He was declined the position with the reason that he didn't have much consulting experience. It was agreed that the company would evaluate his performance for a year or two and then promote him. Goran accepted the offer. He was successful in negotiating the salary in the lower to mid range of that of a senior consulting manager, though he was offered the manager's position.

A start date three months away was agreed with the HR. Goran was excited to onboard. The first two days were the mandatory onboarding session he had to attend, where he learned more about the company, its projects, and its clients. Even before Goran started, it was decided by the management that he would be working on the telco client account on a cloud project. However, just a few weeks before his onboarding, the telco cloud project manager who interviewed him, left the company.

On the third day of his new job, Goran received an e-mail from another project manager named Alisa (name changed) if he wanted to work on the operations support system (OSS) project for the same telco client. OSS manages the network operations services such as service activation, service assurance, service fulfillment, data mediation, and inventory management. There were two assistant project managers in her team. One of them named Karan (name changed) was going on parental leave in the next two weeks for three months. Alisa wanted Goran to urgently fill up the position as she could not find any other resources. Goran explained to her that he did not have the required experience with OSS and was not the right fit for the position. However, Alisa reassured him that the position needed transferable skills such as project management and stakeholder management only and did not require any technical OSS skills. Goran did not find the scope of the project very appealing, which involved the operational management of the old legacy OSS systems. He was obviously interested in cloud, data, AI, and generative AI, the latest hot technologies in the market. Goran who was just three days old in the company did not want to look bad by saying an immediate *no* to Alisa. Instead, he negotiated time till the end of the week to reply with his decision.

Meanwhile, on the telco cloud project, a new project manager named Sandhya (name changed) was hired. Goran immediately reached out to Sandhya and expressed his interest in joining her team. However, he was told that the project was going through some major escalations and the hiring was on hold for the moment, until the internal client account management team meeting on Wednesday, the next week.

It was 4 pm, Wednesday, the next week. Goran pinged Sandhya on Microsoft (MS) teams to find out about the meeting status. He got to know that the meeting was rescheduled to Monday at 3 pm, the following week. Goran's reponse to Alisa was pending and overdue and he began receiving frequent emails from her asking him about his decision. He bought more time from her until the following Monday, the close of business.

Monday, next week at 4 pm, Goran pinged Sandhya once again. There was no response from her. He dropped her an e-mail. No response. Goran waited until 6 pm that evening hoping to receive a response. There was no response. The next day at around 1 pm, he received an e-mail from Sandhya that he was hired on the project and had to sign a few nondisclosure agreement forms for the client. He immediately replied with all the formalities. In return, he received a few introductory project documents, access to the project SharePoint, and a couple of meeting invites. He was all set to get started on the project he longed for. He wrote an e-mail to Alisa about his decision not to join her project and thanked her for considering him for this opportunity.

At around 4 pm, just three hours after his hiring, Goran received an upsetting e-mail from Sandhya that he would be no longer working on the telco cloud project with her. Instead, he would be on the OSS project as per the decision by the client account management team. He should touch base with Alisa immediately to work on the next steps. Goran immediately called up Sandhya. She had no explanation. She told him to reach out to John (name changed), one of the leaders and decision makers in the client account management team if he has any questions. Within moments of hanging up the phone call with Sandhya, Alisa pinged Goran. There was no *hi* nor *hello*. She wrote:

You are assigned to OSS legacy project on account priority. Please touch base with Karan for handover.

Goran was disappointed. He looked up John in MS teams for his number. His status showed red: *In a meeting*. Goran waited till 6 pm. Finally, he saw a green dot next to John's name, showing his availability. Goran called up John and tried to explain that he was not a good fit for OSS and would like to work on telco cloud project instead.

John said:

We know that you don't have OSS skills. But if you don't join Alisa, it will be impossible for us to deliver. You just need to be in this role for three months until Karan returns from his parental leave.

Goran was speechless. He couldn't argue much with John, his senior. With a heavy heart, he hung up the phone. He tried to reach the head of communications practice. His status showed: *On a vacation, will return on Monday, the next week.* Goran called up the senior colleague, who interviewed him and explained the entire situation. He said, "It always happens in the world of consulting. Things are very dynamic and ad hoc. Take it up for the team."

Goran met Karan the next day for the handover. Karan was very helpful and friendly. He walked him through all the project details and introduced him to other members of the team. He forwarded all the internal team meeting invites along with the important weekly status update meeting with the customer. On his final day before the leave, Karan scheduled a lunch meeting with the customer and invited Goran to meet them in person. Karan introduced, "Meet Goran. He will be replacing me as the assistant project manager." Goran was glad to meet the customer but was a bit surprised that Karan did not say he would be temporarily replacing him. After the lunch meeting, Goran met Karan in private and told him that he should have been clearer with the introduction. Karan had thought that Goran was his permanent replacement. Karan called up Alisa. She replied that she was not aware that Goran was temporary. To clear up the confusion, Goran called up John, taking Alisa and Karan in the loop. John assured him that he was a temporary replacement, and Karan would take up the position after he came back from parental leave. Karan's face fell off.

Two weeks into the OSS legacy project, Goran realized that he was not adding much value to the internal team and the customer meetings due to his lack of OSS knowledge. He realized his position was not as critical as John explained to him over the phone, "it would be impossible to deliver if you don't join." The technical team leads in the OSS project could have stepped up to take over the project and the stakeholder management responsibilities temporarily until Karan returned. The other assistant project manager named Petri (name changed) could have shared the load too. Goran felt his position was redundant. He could have been more motivated and added more value to the telco cloud project that matched his skills and interests. Goran brought it up before Alisa. But to his disappointment, she told Goran that he needed to ramp up the OSS skills to add more value.

Goran had no interest nor motivation to learn the OSS skills for old legacy systems. It was not what he had initially agreed with Alisa.

He called up John. John echoed Alisa's words.

He called the senior colleague. He said, "In consulting, the scope of work can change. One needs to be flexible."

He then scheduled a meeting with the head of communications practice, who said:

> Just stay on the OSS legacy project. You are just a few weeks old. You are new to OSS, new to the company, and new to the client account. Take this project as a good step to know the account well.

"But I want to work on cloud, data, and AI. That's my interest and I believe that's what I was initially hired for." said Goran.

"In that case, I have a suggestion for you. You can work with the sales team. They have some new generative AI projects in the pipeline."

The suggestion was convincing. Goran reached out to the sales team. It was very disoriented and spaced out. They had no pipeline in place and had no plans to implement generative AI. Goran had a few meetings with the sales team. But things went in circles with no clear outcome and ownership. Goran was getting frustrated.

Next week, Goran met Sandhya at the customer site. They both had lunch together. He asked how the telco cloud project was going. She replied that they were in need of resources. Goran's role was still open. It was very difficult to find someone with cloud, data, and AI skills and a telco background, both from within the company and externally. Goran told Sandhya that he was working only 50 percent of his time on the OSS legacy project and asked if he could work 50 percent on her project. Sandhya was fine with that. Goran called up John and asked if he could split his time evenly on both projects. This way he could keep his motivation going, and it would be a possible win–win for both teams. John was fine with that if Alisa was ok.

The next day, Goran called up Alisa. She said, "No. I want you 100 percent on the OSS legacy project."

"But you know I work only 50 percent of my time. The remaining 50 percent I sit idle." said Goran.

"In that case, I can give you more work. There is a lot of invoicing work that needs to be done. Work with the finance." replied Alisa.

"But that is not part of my job. You hired me for stakeholder and project management. And now you want me to do finance work." argued Goran.

"Let me talk to John and get back to you." said Alisa. She hung up the call.

Alisa didn't call back. The next day Goran called her.

"Please, Alisa! I request you. It would be great if you could allow me 50 percent on telco cloud." pleaded Goran. "They need resources too."

"If they need resources, it's the management problem. Not your problem." said Alisa angrily. "I don't want any further discussion on this. You might have all the time. But for me, every minute is important."

"But please try to understand. I spoke to John. He is ok, if you are ok." implored Goran.

"You are just thinking about your interest. And I know what you will do if I allow you 50 percent. You will ditch the OSS legacy project and spend more time on the telco cloud." said Alisa.

That was the end for Goran. His frustration had reached its peak.

"You are now questioning my integrity." said Goran.

"Do you want to work on this project?" asked Alisa.

"Yes, but 50 percent. And 50 percent on the telco cloud." replied Goran.

"Again I am asking, do you want to work 100 percent on this project or not?" yelled Alisa.

"No!" replied Goran.

"Alright."

Alisa hung up the phone. Goran pinged John saying he wanted to meet him urgently. He happened to be on the customer site. John scheduled a meeting at 3 pm.

Goran said:

Things are not going well between me and Alisa. I do not wish to continue on this project. Things can only get worse if I continue. I don't want it to impact our team and the customers. I am sorry!

John was upset. He replied, "That's not how we work. I feel very sorry for Alisa. This abandonment from you is not professional."

"I am sorry once again. But I can assure you that my quitting won't impact the delivery." replied Goran.

John called up Alisa if it was ok if Goran rolled off. She was fine.

The news that Goran left the OSS legacy project spread among the team. He received a couple of pings from his other teammates. Goran called up Sandhya to let her know that he was available for the telco cloud project.

She replied:

I am sorry. We have already hired someone for the position.

What is the main problem here? It is a lack of *empathy*, because of which the team was unable to connect and communicate effectively. The team was just expected to deliver, without understanding how they felt. Everyone on the team had inner motives. Alisa wanted a promotion very badly. She was just focused on the numbers and cared less to motivate her team. Karan was demotivated and wanted to move to some other project. He had brought it up twice before Alisa and John. His request was turned down saying that there was no one to replace him. He decided to take advantage of the labor law and use his pending parental leave as an excuse to get out of the project to which Alisa couldn't object. He proposed Goran as his replacement. Karan knew his team could manage without him, and his position was redundant. But he didn't bring it up before Alisa. As a result, Alisa panicked when Karan was leaving. She passed her panic over to John, whose focus was to keep the customer happy. He felt it would be impossible to deliver if the position remains unfilled, which would affect customer satisfaction. He didn't bother to know what motivated Goran and where could he bring good customer value. Also, the senior colleague and the head of communications practice didn't really support Goran either due to the risk of jeopardizing their relationship with John's client account management team.

Had the team been more empathetic, Karan could have moved out to a new project. OSS team leads could have stepped up to take more responsibility. Alisa could have allowed Goran 50 percent on the telco cloud. John could have backed up her decision. And Goran would have been happy, motivated, and more productive.

Empathy is the ability to understand other people's emotions. It is about understanding what others think, feel, and will (desire).

There are three distinct types of empathy: cognitive empathy, emotional empathy, and empathic concern:[1]

Cognitive empathy is the ability to understand another person's perspective or simply understand what other people think *(Think)*. *Emotional* empathy is the ability to feel what someone else feels *(Feel)*. *Empathic concern* is the ability to sense what other person needs from you *(Will)*.

THINK	**FEEL**	**WILL**
Ability to understand another person's perspective	Ability to feel what someone else feels	Ability to sense what another person needs from you

Figure 3.1 Think–Feel–Will

Digital transformation projects require one to work in teams. A team is more likely to perform better when people are more connected and empathetic toward each other. It is the responsibility of a digital leader to drive empathy in an organization.

Types of People

Before we practice empathy at work, it is important to understand the types of people and what motivates them. There are five types of people at work: type 1, type 2, type 3, type 4, and type 5.

- For type 1, work is never a priority. They can be valuable employees often dependable and hardworking, but their focus is elsewhere, on their family or hobbies or some creative pursuits. These are the staff you will find mainly in administrative or in the back office. They often work hard because their work provides them with security in their personal life.
- Type 2 care deeply about the social purpose of work, which is changing the world. They think, are we building something that will last? Programmers, technologists, architects, and engineers are the ones who belong to such a category.
- Type 3 are motivated by a sense of stability and progress and flourish when companies offer them a clear plan to develop and grow over time.

Type 1	Work is never a priority	Motivated by hobbies, pursuits, etc.
Type 2	World-changers	Care deeply about social purpose
Type 3	Personal growth and development	Motivated by stability and progress
Type 4	Team-oriented	Collaboration with others
Type 5	Risk-takers	Lose BIG or Win BIG

Figure 3.2 5 Types of people at work

- Type 4 are team-oriented and motivated by collaboration with others.
- Type 5 are the risk takers that want to know they are pushing it to the limits. They recognize they could lose big, but they are attracted to the idea that they could win big.

Type 2 or the world changers and Type 5 or the risk takers are the best types of people for enabling digital transformation. The best way to motivate these categories is to offer them autonomy and recognition.[2]

4D Model

There is another four dimensional or 4D model that classifies people into the following four types: dreamers, designers, doubters, and doers.

| Dreamers | Designers | Doubters | Doers |

Figure 3.3 4D model

Dreamers are the ones that dream about the future without worrying much about the past.

Designers are the ones who take the dream further and design what is possible.

Doubters are the ones that are skeptical in a positive sense and are persuaded by facts, proof of concepts, and data before they decide to invest in these ideas.

Doers are the ones who put these ideas into scale.

People are very important part of a business. If you understand their needs and develop them, they will be motivated and more loyal to you, which will enable you to achieve results. But if you only focus on numbers and care less about people, they will leave you, which will cause the numbers to go down.

One of my batchmates Sean (name changed) who studied master's in telecommunications and networking with me at the University of Pennsylvania, after graduation in the year 2007, got a job as an analyst, with a mid sized IT consulting firm based in Philadelphia. The CEO of the company was a very ambitious leader with an autocratic leadership style. He was a taskmaster, with a strong focus on the numbers. His style trickled down the corporate hierarchy and became a standard way of working for the lower management.

On his first day, Sean was asked to report at 8 am at the client's office. He wore business formals, a standard dress code of the consultants. But out of excitement and anxiety, he forgot to wear a tie. He was greeted by his project manager who had been there much earlier. The first thing he noticed was Sean's missing tie. He was sent home and asked to report back wearing a tie. When Sean came back, he was introduced to the team and the clients, had an introductory phone call with HR, and was immediately sucked into the project. In the evening, there was a team dinner which lasted till 11 pm. By the time, he reached home, it was midnight. He was expected to report at 7 am, the next day. When he arrived, he received his manager's note that he was in a workshop with the client till 4 pm and would meet afterward. Sean's meeting with his manager lasted till 6 pm, where he was given some tasks and clear instructions on how to deliver them. Sean asked his manager if he could complete them before noon tomorrow.

To his disappointment, his manager replied, "Do them now."

Sean stayed in the office till 10 pm. He left for home after he finished his task. He was super tired. On reaching home, he just crashed on his bed.

This became his daily routine. He was asked to report at 7 am. He almost sat idle until 3 pm, waiting for his manager to finish the meeting with the client and give him more tasks. Then he stayed up late finishing them. Sean had no personal life left. He was slowly getting frustrated and demotivated.

After a few weeks, the project load increased. He was asked to work on the weekends too. His frustration reached its peak when he received a call from his manager on a Sunday evening, while he was watching the famous Super Bowl final between the New York Giants and New England Patriots, considered to be one of the best games of all time. His manager was in the office, busy with a delivery report. Sean was asked to come and assist him.

It was a very difficult transition for Sean from his school life to rigorous corporate life. The work culture was very demanding and toxic. Most of his colleagues had left the company. Eventually, his manager was able to meet the deadlines and make the customer happy but at the cost of demotivated and dissatisfied employees. It was a victory, but without honor. Sean was a *type 2* and a *doer*. However, he was not recognized and utilized properly by his company. A few months after the project was over, he left.

Link Between Empathy and Profitability

Researchers at Harvard Business School developed a model that established a link between motivation, employee productivity, and company profitability. Customer loyalty drives profitability. Customer satisfaction drives customer loyalty. Values drive customer satisfaction. Employee productivity drives values. Employee loyalty drives employee productivity. Employee satisfaction drives employee loyalty. And motivation drives employee satisfaction.

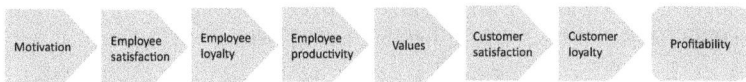

Figure 3.4 Link between motivation and profitability

There is one more link that can be added—empathy drives motivation.

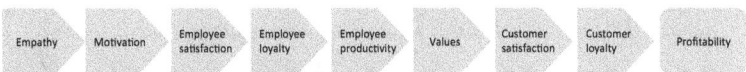

Figure 3.5 The empathy link

From Figure 3.5, we can see how empathy is linked to profitability.

The WhatsApp Experiment

One of my friends, let us call him Ram, got phished and had his LinkedIn profile hacked. The hacker deleted the account and his page no longer existed. Suddenly, Ram lost his valuable network of professionals he built over a decade. He was disappointed. His only option left was to rebuild the network. He created a new LinkedIn profile, and I was the first one to accept his connection request. He knew that I was writing a book, and I remembered him asking me once if he could be of any help to me. So, I asked if he could help me collect some data for my research on empathy, while he rebuilds his LinkedIn network. He volunteered.

Ram had a big network of 526 people on WhatsApp. From the list, he selected 225 people whom he wanted to add on LinkedIn. Ram had recently changed his WhatsApp number. He was not sure how many people in his network would recognize the new number, although they could recognize his picture associated with it. I asked him to broadcast the following message to all and make a note of how many people respond:

www.linkedin.com/in/<Ram's username> Hello, I am rebuilding my LinkedIn network. For some reason, people are not getting my requests. Would be great if you could send me a connection request.

After a wait time of 24 hours, to those who did not respond and send a connection request, Ram sent another message:

Hello <name of the receiver>, how are you? Are you OK to send me a connection request?

After a wait time of 48 hours, to those who did not respond and send a connection request, Ram sent another message:

Hello <name of the receiver>, hope you are doing fine. My LinkedIn account got hacked recently and I lost the valuable network, I built over a decade. I want to rebuild my connections fast as I need them very frequently. I have a weekly limit for sending new requests. I want to save it to send requests to those whom I don't know as well as you. I would appreciate if you could help me achieve my objective. Regards, Ram

After a week, it was observed that:

- To the first message, only 12 people (5 percent) clicked on the link and sent a connection request within 24 hours.
- To the second message, 49 people (21 percent) clicked on the link and sent a connection request within 48 hours.
- To the third message, 65 people (29 percent) clicked on the link and sent a connection request within a week.
- 99 people (45 percent) did not respond at all.

After the exercise, all the participants were asked to fill out a multiple choice survey anonymously answering questions related to think, feel, and will.

The multiple choice options were different for different respondents for *think* and *feel* as shown in Figure 3.6 and 3.7 respectively. However, they were same for all respondents for *will* as shown in Figure 3.8.

Response to the first message:

Out of 12 respondents,

7 selected: I must help him.
3 selected: Why didn't he send me a request through LinkedIn directly?
1 selected: But we were already connected on LinkedIn.
1 selected: Other.

Response to the second message:

Out of 49 respondents,

17 selected: I must help him.
13 selected: Let me check his profile on LinkedIn first.
16 selected: Why is he rebuilding his network?
3 selected: Other.

Response to the third message:

Out of 65 respondents,

45 selected: I must help him now.
16 selected: Let me check his profile on LinkedIn first.

Think

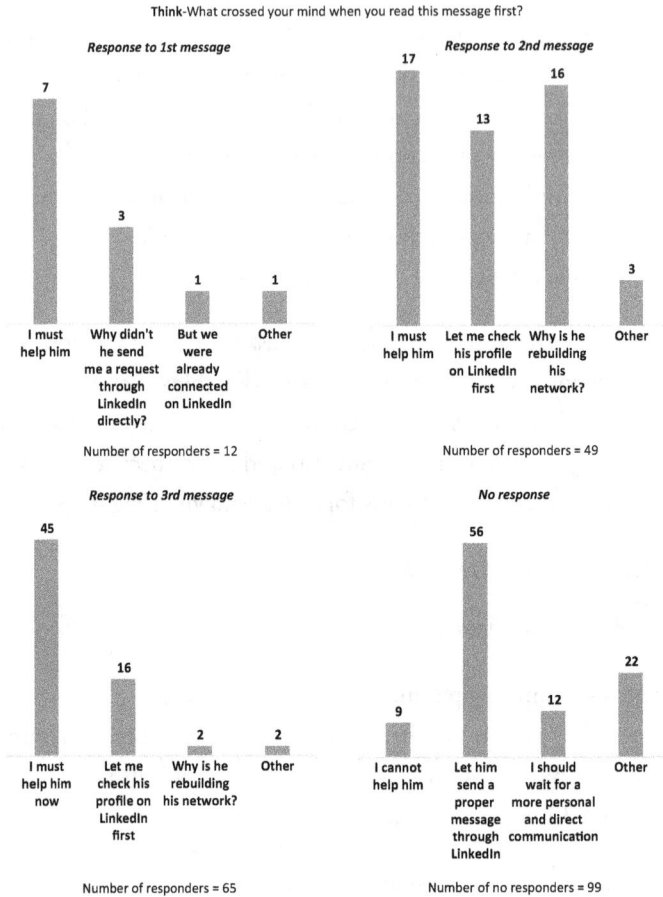

Think-What crossed your mind when you read this message first?

Figure 3.6 **Think: What crossed your mind when you read this message first?**

2 selected: Why is he rebuilding his network?
2 selected: Other.

No response:

Out of 99 nonrespondents,

9 selected: I cannot help him.
56 selected: Let him send me a proper request through LinkedIn.
12 selected: I should wait for more personal and direct communication from him such as phone call, in person meeting, and so on.
22 selected: Other.

Feel

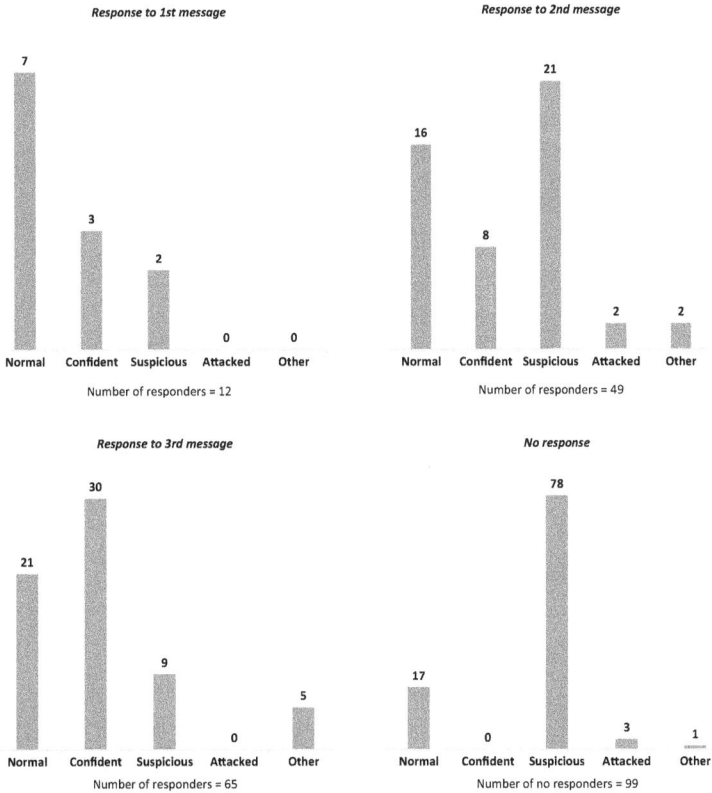

Response to 1st message

Number of responders = 12

Response to 2nd message

Number of responders = 49

Response to 3rd message

Number of responders = 65

No response

Number of no responders = 99

Figure 3.7 Feel: How did you feel about it?

Response to the first message:

Out of 12 respondents, 7 felt normal, 3 felt confident, and 2 felt suspicious.

Response to the second message:

Out of 49 respondents, 16 felt normal, 8 felt confident, 21 felt suspicious, 2 felt attacked, 2 had other feelings.

Response to the third message:

Out of 65 respondents, 21 felt normal, 30 felt confident, 9 felt suspicious, 5 had other feelings.

No response:

Out of 99 nonrespondents, 17 felt normal, 78 felt suspicious, 3 felt attacked, and 1 had other feelings.

Will

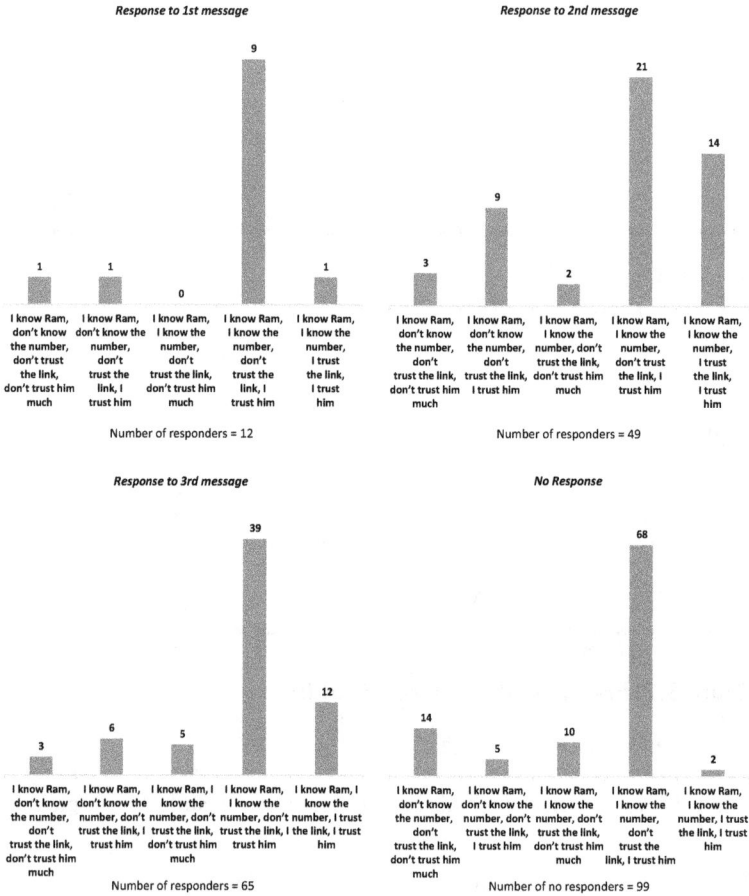

Figure 3.8 Will: Why did you click on the connection request?

Options	Respondents to the first message	Respondents to the second message	Respondents to the third message	Non respondents
I know Ram, don't know the number, don't trust the link, don't trust him much	1	3	3	14
I know Ram, don't know the number, don't trust the link, I trust him	1	9	6	5

Options	Respondents to the first message	Respondents to the second message	Respondents to the third message	Non respondents
I know Ram, I know the number, don't trust the link, don't trust him much	0	2	5	10
I know Ram, I know the number, don't trust the link, I trust him	9	21	39	68
I know Ram, I know the number, I trust the link, I trust him	1	14	12	2
Total	12	49	65	99

The participants were asked to select the most applicable statement. Figure 3.9 shows their response:

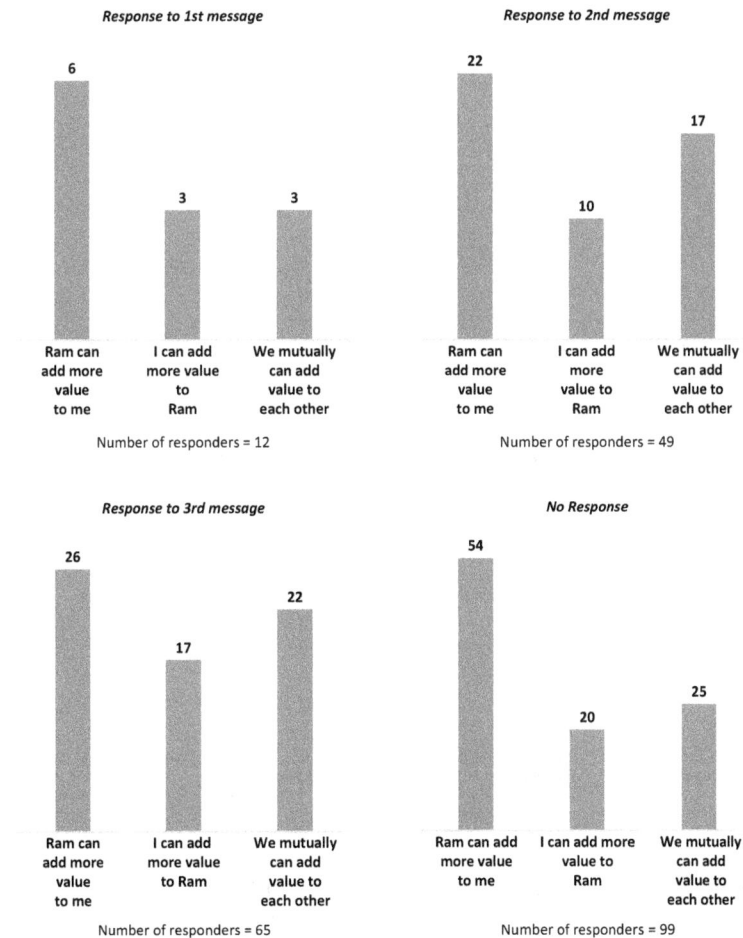

Figure 3.9 *Which statement is most applicable?*

Options	Respondents to the first message	Respondents to the second message	Respondents to the third message	Non respondents
Ram can add more value to me	6	22	26	54
I can add more value to Ram	3	10	17	20
We mutually can add value to each other	3	17	22	25
Total	12	49	65	99

The participants were asked to describe their relationship with Ram. Figure 3.10 shows their response:

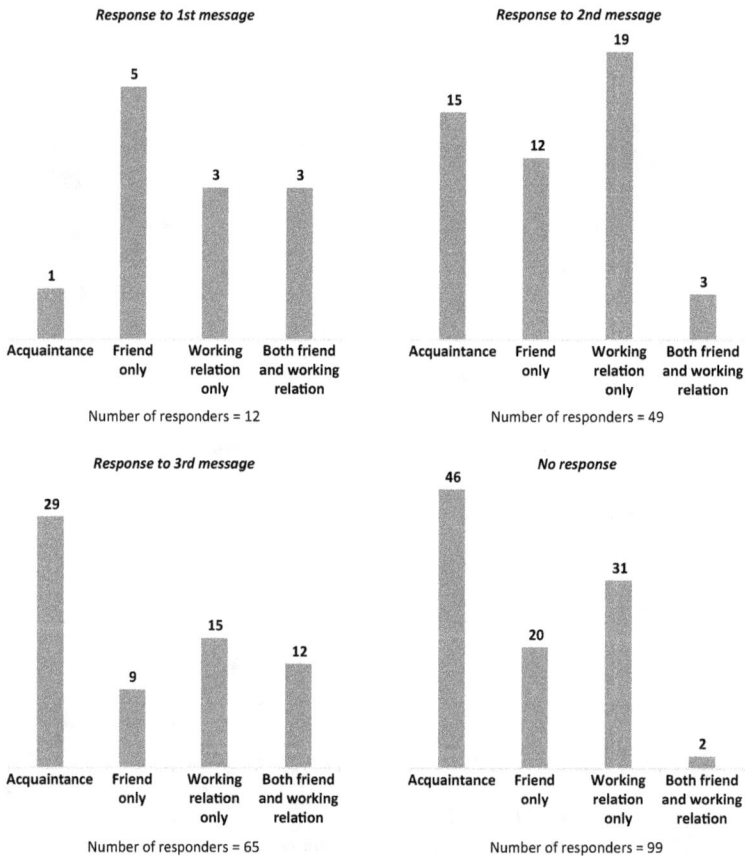

Figure 3.10 *How do you best describe the relationship with Ram?*

Options	Respondents to the first message	Respondents to the second message	Respondents to the third message	Non respondents
Acquaintance	1	15	29	46
Friend only	5	12	9	20
Working relation only	3	19	15	31
Both friend and working relation	3	3	12	2
Total	12	49	65	99

Some additional questions were asked to the nonresponders:

- Were you or anyone from your family or friends phished before? Figure 3.11 shows the response.
- Rate your awareness level on cyber security and data protection on a scale of 1 to 10, 1:lowest, 10:highest. Figure 3.12 shows the response.

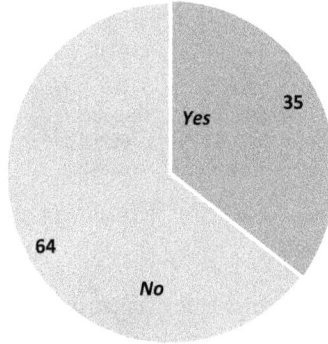

Number of responders = 99

Figure 3.11 Response

The first message was worded very much like a phishing scam. To which, only 12 out of 225 people (5 percent) clicked the link. Among those who clicked the link, 11 (91 percent) had trust in Ram because an equal number of them identified themselves as friends, colleagues, and both. Further, 10 (83 percent) felt normal and confident, and 9 (75 percent) thought him to be a value add.

To the second message, 49 out of 225 people (21 percent) clicked the link. Among those who clicked the link, 44 (89 percent) had trust in Ram, and 34 (69 percent) identified themselves as friends, colleagues, and both. Also, 24 (48 percent) felt normal and confident. 39 (79 percent) think him to be a value add.

Rate your awareness on cyber security and data
protection on a scale of 1 to 10, 1:lowest and 10:highest

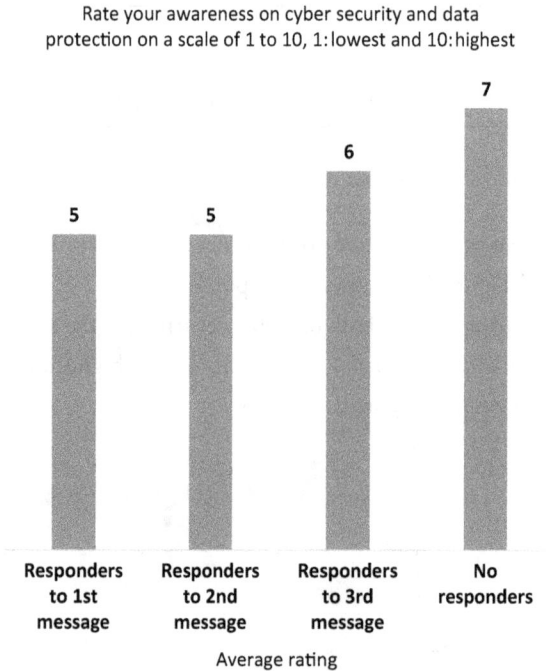

Figure 3.12 Response

To the third message, which was detailed and personalized, 65 out of 225 people (29 percent) clicked the link. Among those who clicked the link, 57 (87 percent) trusted him, and 36 (55 percent) identified them as his friends, colleagues, or both. 51 (78 percent) felt normal and confident, and 48 (73 percent) thought him to be a value add.

99 out of 225 people (45 percent) who did not respond, 78 (78 percent approximately) were suspicious and 68 (68 percent approximately) felt Ram should reach out to them through a more trusted channel. Further, 75 (75 percent approximately) trust him, and 79 (79 percent approximately) feel him to be a value add. In addition, 53 (53 percent approximately) think him to be a friend, colleague, or both. Then, 35 percent of them responded *yes* if they or anyone they knew had been phished before. Also, the average rating of awareness on cyber security and data

protection was highest among the nonresponders, which led to their decision of not clicking the link.

We see that 187 out of 225 people trust Ram. So, the level of trust in Ram is high—83 percent. 175 out of 225 people, which is 77 percent consider him to be a value add. Further, 134 out of 225 people, which is 59 percent identify themselves as his friend, colleagues, and both. There was lesser response to his first message as it was not worded empathetically. If Ram had sent the third message in place of first one, there would have been higher chances of more people clicking the link.

From this experiment, we conclude that people due to some biases, doubts, or previous experiences, think and feel in a certain way. A leader should be more empathetic while communicating. A less empathetic personal communication with poorly worded messages will not motivate people to take action and get the desired results. This will have a negative impact on the business.

Manager and the Team Member Experiment

Another experiment was conducted with 20 people who were split into two groups: A and B of ten each. In each group, they were further divided into five pairs. Each pair had to do a roleplay of a manager and a team member. The following briefs were given to the manager and the team members in each pair. They were given five minutes to go through their respective briefs. Some special instructions were given to both in the end.

Manager Brief

You are a manager of a high-performing team, where every team member is working to the best of his/her capability. Your customer is difficult to manage. You need full commitment from your team to meet its expectations. There is one team member who had been transferred from another team three months ago. He is not working with the same commitment level. He takes a longer time to get the job done and has made a few mistakes repeatedly. He is not volunteering to take up ownership, bring in new ideas, and connect with the rest of the team. Some of the team members have brought up this issue to you. They feel he is not contributing enough. Your job as a manager is to motivate him and turn his performance around. How would you do it?

Instructions

- Try to keep the conversation as professional as possible.
- Do not seek personal information from the team member.
- Your objective is to motivate the team member and increase his commitment level. Use all sorts of tactics to motivate him. You are allowed to be direct and issue threats if necessary.

Team Member Brief

It has been three months since you have been moved into a new team. You were not happy with the management's decision to move you there in the first place. But then you had no other alternatives and had to accept their decision against your will. Although you appreciate the energy and commitment of your colleagues toward work, you feel you are not a good fit for the team. People in the team just talk about work and most of the time work till late evenings. This has affected your work-life balance. You want to finish work within the office hours to go home and spend time with your pregnant spouse. You do not like what you do and do not feel motivated to work for longer hours. Your manager has just sent you an invite for a one-to-one meeting for tomorrow without mentioning the agenda. This has never happened before. But you can guess that your manager wants to discuss this issue with you.

Instructions

- Try to keep the conversation as professional as possible.
- Try to resist the demands and suggestions politely made by the manager, wherever needed.
- Do not share your personal problems and situation with your manager.

The manager and the team member in each pair then had a meeting for five minutes. After that, they took a break and answered the following questions confidentially:

- How do I feel about the meeting?
- What do I think about the other person?
- What does the other person need from me?

- Is the other person able to understand me?
- How can the person understand me better?

Now, the managers in Group B were made to read the team member brief privately without letting the team members know. New instructions were provided to Group B managers:

- Try to keep the conversation as professional as possible.
- Be kind and considerate with the team member.

The one-to-one meetings in each pair were continued for another five minutes. In the end, both answered the same preceding questions confidentially.

The team members in each group were asked to fill in additional two questions at the end:

- Rate your motivation level on a scale of 1 to 10
- Rate your commitment level on a scale of 1 to 10
  (1: lowest, 10: highest)

It was observed that the first five minutes of the meeting did not go as per expectations for the pairs in both groups. The level of disagreement was high. There was a mutual feeling of distrust. The managers expected the team members to cooperate with them and show motivation and commitment to the project. The team members felt that the managers just wanted them to deliver without caring how they felt. All the pairs started the conversations on friendly terms initially. But when the team members didn't budge, the managers slowly started using threats. The conversations got more alienated and difficult.

In the next five minutes of the meeting, in Group A, most of the conversations became more forceful. Some even ran into arguments. Not even a single pair reached an agreement. In Group B, the face of conversations totally changed. The managers showed kindness and consideration. They began inquiring about the health and well-being of the employees and listened to their problems attentively. A team member in one pair even openly shared a personal problem with the respective manager. All the pairs were able to reach an agreement.

The average rating for motivation and commitment was higher in Group B than Group A.

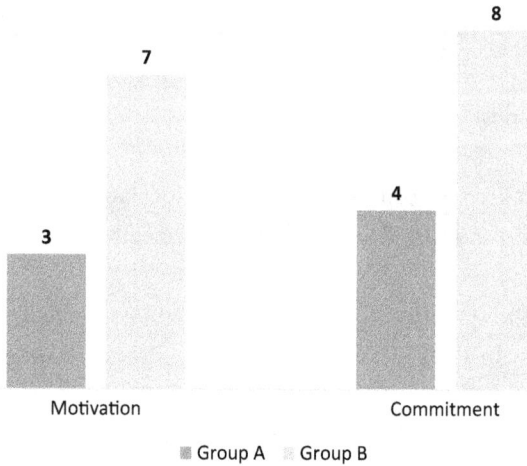

Figure 3.13 Comparison

This experiment shows that empathy is critical in motivating employees to get the work done. If the performance of an employee is poor at work, most of the managers tell the employees what needs to be done to improve the performance within a specific timeline. Very few ask the employees how they feel about it. There might be many things going on in the private life of an employee—sick kids, relationship issues, financial crises, and so on, which will have an impact on the performance at work. Empathy is about showing care and concern for the people. Simon Sinek said:

Leaders are often so concerned about their status and position in the organization, that they actually forget what their real job is. The real job of a leader is not being in charge but taking care of those in our charge.

Cultivating Empathy

The following are the 5 steps for cultivating empathy:

Step 1: Assess your empathy

Step 2: Collect data about the person/people you want to empathize with

Step 3: Analysis of Think–Feel–Will

Step 4: Communication using active listening principles

Step 5: Observe your progress with empathy over 12 weeks

Step 1: Assess your empathy

The following assessment contains 20 statements. Based on how closely you agree with them, give the following rating on a scale of 1 to 5, 5: strongly agree, 4: agree, 3: neutral, 2: disagree, 1: strongly disagree.

#	Statements	Rating
1	More than laying people off, it is important how you lay them off.	
2	I often tend to listen more than I speak.	
3	I like developing people.	
4	I often share credit with others for success.	
5	I am better at influencing people at work.	
6	I get influenced by great people easily.	
7	I manage my stakeholder relationships effectively.	
8	I spend lots of time and effort in building my professional network.	
9	I feel uncomfortable when one of my team members feels demotivated at work.	
10	Before giving negative feedback to someone at work, I try to imagine how I would feel if I were in their place.	
11	I know what motivates my team and how to motivate them.	
12	I cannot tolerate disrespectful behavior in the workplace.	
13	I share other's motivation and enthusiasm.	
14	I feel bad when deserving employees don't get what they deserve.	
15	I can easily understand other's views and perspectives.	
16	I still seek input and opinions from others, even though I know the solution to a problem.	
17	I like to help my colleagues at work.	
18	I like to work in a team.	
19	I deliver on commitments.	
20	I value mine and other people's time.	
	Average score	

Use the following table to map your empathy level:

Score range	Empathy level
Average score > 4.5	Very high
4 < Average score ≤ 4.5	High
3 < Average score ≤ 4	Medium
2 < Average score ≤ 3	Low
1 < Average score ≤ 2	Very low
Average score < 1	Negligible

If your empathy score is greater than 4, you have it in you. It would be still beneficial to follow the following framework. But if it is less than 4, you certainly need to follow the framework to cultivate it further.

Step 2: Collect data about the person/people you want to empathize with

Use the following sheet:

Data	Responses
Name of the person	
Gender	
Title	
Number of years in the company	
Working relation to you (direct report, customer, manager, executive, etc.)	
What is the environment in which you interact (office, remote, hybrid)?	
What type does the person belong to (type 1, 2, 3, 4, or 5)?	
As per the 4D model, how do you categorize the person?	
Why do you want to empathize with the person?	
How important is the relationship to you?	
What positive impact would it have on your business?	
How can you mutually benefit from each other?	

Step 3: Analysis of Think–Feel–Will

Try to get answers to the following questions by observing the person yourself first. You can also get answers from other people who know the person. Replace *x* with your real event or incidence. Feel free to add more questions to the following list if needed:

Think	
Questions	Response
What is the person thinking about the business/project/current situation?	
What is the person's perspective about me?	
What is the person's perspective about other people?	
Does the person have an opinion?	
Will the person's perspective about the business/project/current situation change after event x happens?	
Will the person's perspective about me change after event x happens?	
Will the person's perspective about other people change after event x happens?	

Feel	
Questions	Response
What is the person feeling about the business/project/current situation?	
How does the person feel about me (good, bad, or neutral feelings)?	
How does the person feel about other people (good, bad, or neutral feelings)?	
Will the person's feelings about the business/project/current situation change after event x happens?	
Will the person's feelings about me change after event x happens?	
Will the person's feelings about other people change after event x happens?	

Will	
Questions	Response
What does the person need from the business/project/current situation?	
What does the person need from me?	
What does the person need from other people?	
Will the person's needs from the business/project/current situation change after event x happens?	
Will the person's needs from me change after event x happens?	
Will the person's needs from other people change after event x happens?	

Step 4: Communication with active listening principles

You can understand better what the person thinks, feels, and wills when you communicate with him/her. Use active listening principles to empathize better. See Appendix 1 for more details.

Step 5: Observe your progress with empathy over 12 weeks

Use the following sheet:

Weeks	Empathy toward the person (Are you able to understand the person?) (Rating 1 to 10, 1: lowest, 10: highest)	What can you do better?
Week 1		
Week 2		
Week 3		
Week 4		
Week 5		
Week 6		
Week 7		
Week 8		
Week 9		
Week 10		
Week 11		
Week 12		

You can practice cultivating empathy through roleplays. See Appendix 2 for more details.

Satya's Empathy at Microsoft

Satya Nadella is a great example of enhancing innovation at Microsoft through a culture of empathy.[3] In his first year, Satya, instead of focusing on the numbers, spent much of his time listening and learning from others. He met with leaders, partners, and customers together with his team and organized focus groups to hear from hundreds of employees across the company. Their feedback indicated that they wanted a CEO who would make changes but respect Microsoft's original ideals, would frequently communicate what was going on, and make Microsoft cool again. He traveled around the globe visiting various customers and Microsoft offices. He also met common people to see how Microsoft technology impacted their lives. He visited schools and even far-out places such as a solar-powered shipping container in Kenya that served as an Internet cafe to listen and experience how customers used Microsoft offerings.

Satya wanted a leadership team that would lean into each other's problems, promote dialogue, and be effective. A team that would align on mission, strategy, and culture. He encouraged his leadership team to read Marshall Rosenberg's book *Nonviolent Communication: A Language of Life: Life-Changing Tools for Healthy Relationships*. It was a clear indication that Satya was going to focus on transforming not only the business strategy but the culture as well. He emphasized how empathy had helped him shape his life and how he had been inspired by the empathy of others, including high-school computer students who had helped his son with special needs with programming software that allowed him to flip through his music selection on the wheelchair. Another example was a project at Microsoft to give people suffering from amyotrophic lateral sclerosis and cerebral palsy more independence through eye-tracking technology.

Satya had to make some tough choices that apparently seemed non-empathic. Microsoft's acquisition of Nokia's mobile business under the tenure of Ballmer proved to be a failure. Satya had to make nearly 18,000 employees redundant, of which 12,500 had moved to Microsoft through the Nokia acquisition. He said:

The need for empathy doesn't take away your need for making hard calls, but you should carry out those decisions with empathy.

Satya's focus right from day one was to position Microsoft as a leader in cloud and mobile. This meant embracing an open innovation model and forming new strategic partnerships with different players in the industry. In the spring of 2014, despite its arch rivalry with Apple, Microsoft made its MS office available on all iOS devices, including the iPhone and iPad. He chose Peggy Johnson, a senior Qualcomm executive, to forge ties with Microsoft's former Silicon Valley rivals, including Dropbox.

Satya describes his personal journey to becoming the CEO:

I drew on a deep well of emotion ... I had been thinking about my life—my parents, my wife and children, my work. It had been a long journey to this point. My mind went back to earlier days: as a child in India, as a young man emigrating to this country, as a husband and the father of a child with special needs, as an engineer designing technologies that reach billions of people worldwide ... even as an obsessed cricket fan who long ago dreamed of being a professional player. All these parts of me came together in this new role, a role that would call upon all of my passions, skills, and values.

Empathy Applications

With empathy, you can add value in the following four areas: team building, stakeholder management and influencing, networking, mentoring and reverse mentoring.

1. Team Building

With empathy, you can build a high-performing team. In a high-performing team, individuals have specialized expertise and complementary skills. They collaborate and innovate together to produce work at the highest level. The opposite of a high-performing team is a dysfunctional team where there is absence of trust, fear of conflict, lack of commitment, avoidance of accountability, and inattention to results.

The Drexler Sibbet model of team building is shown in Figure 3.14.

It can be viewed as a bouncing ball in the form of V. The left side is creating, and the right side is sustaining. The left side is about preparation and putting efforts into building the team, and the right side shows the performance or reaping the results. The harder you throw the ball on the ground, the higher it rises.

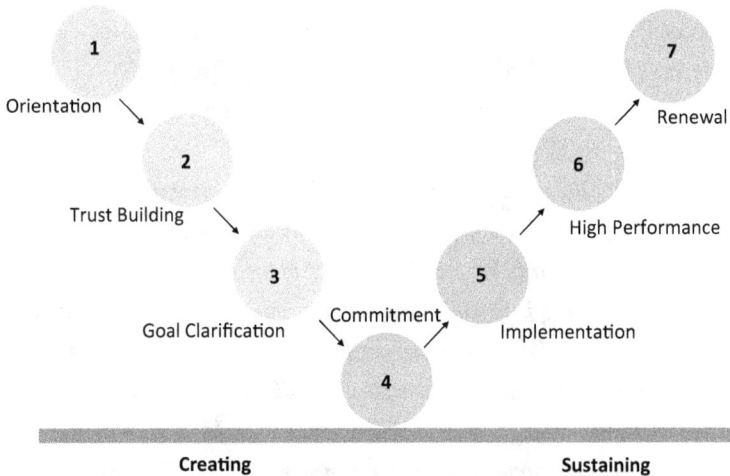

Figure 3.14 The Drexler Sibbet model

Activity

Do the think–feel–will analysis with your team using the following sheet:

Data	Team Member 1	Team Member 2	...Team Member n
Name of the person			
Gender			
Title			
Number of years in the company			
Working relation to you (direct report, customer, manager, executive, etc.)			
What is the environment in which you interact (office, remote, hybrid)?			
What type does the person belong to (Type 1, 2, 3, 4, or 5)?			
As per the 4D model, how do you categorize the person?			
Why do you want to empathize with the person?			
How important is the relationship to you?			
What positive impact would it have on your business?			
How can you mutually benefit from each other?			

Questions	Team Member 1	Team Member 2	...	Team Member N
Think				
Questions: 1...n				
Feel				
Questions: 1...n				
Will				
Questions: 1...n				

(Continued)

Then use the following steps of the Drexler Sibbet model for team building:

Creating	
Stages	Questions to ask
a. Orientation: At orientation, the teams are at their formative stage. People most often don't see a clear purpose of the project and are unable to understand how their skills can add value. As a leader, you can empathize with your team, clear their doubts, and build relationships.	-How do you feel about being on this team? -What are your expectations from this project/team? -How could your strengths add value to the team? -What are your expectations from me as a leader?
b. Trust building: Without trusting other team members, it would be very difficult to collaborate and share knowledge and ideas.	-Do you trust your team members? How would you rate it on a scale of 1 to 10, 1: lowest and 10: highest? -Do they trust you enough? How would you rate it on a scale of 1 to 10, 1: lowest and 10: highest? -How can we develop trust in our team? -How can I support as a leader to ensure trust building?
c. Goal clarification: Before the project kicks off, it is important to set phases and milestones and to fix the goals and objectives for each team member.	-How do you feel about your objectives? -What do you think about the team objectives? -How would you monitor your individual and team progress?
d. Commitment: A committed and motivated team leads to better results and performance. At this stage, the creation of timelines, deadlines, resource allocations, workstreams or subteams, and execution methodologies (sprints as in agile) takes place.	-How do you feel about the project setup? -How would you accomplish your objectives? Is there any skill development or learning course you need to enroll in to help you accomplish this? -What is your commitment level on a scale of 1 to 10, 1: lowest and 10: highest?
Sustaining	
Stages	Questions to ask
e. Implementation The project execution begins at this stage where the team faces real challenges. There might be high-pressure situations where the team might face burnout. It is your duty as a leader to keep your team motivated and support them toward achieving the objectives.	-How do you feel about the project implementation? -Are there any pending issues to be resolved? -Is there any support you need from me?

Sustaining	
Stages	Questions to ask
f. High performance A team that coordinates well among its members and fulfills customer expectations by delivering with high speed and quality leads to high performance. As they complete every phase and milestone, their motivation and confidence increase.	-What do you value most about our team? -What is that thing you have achieved that you feel proud of? -How can you do better?
g. Renewal It occurs when the team members roll off from the project either toward the end of a milestone or toward the end of a project. As a leader, it is important that you seek their feedback on what worked, what didn't work, and how to do things better.	-What is your overall feeling about the project? -How could we have worked better together? -What feedback do you have for me as a leader? -What lessons will you take away with you?

2. Stakeholder Management and Influencing

With empathy, you would be able to understand the needs and emotions of your stakeholders and manage and influence them better. As a leader of digital transformation projects, you have to deal with different stakeholders. Some may agree, while some may disagree with your ideas. Some may trust you more, and others may trust you less. As per the model suggested by Peter Block, based on the level of trust and agreement, the stakeholders can be categorized into:

- Adversaries
- Opponents
- Bedfellows
- Fence sitters
- Allies

Adversaries have low trust and low agreement with your ideas, decisions, and projects and will try to hinder, delay, or disrupt the progress. They are difficult people to deal with.

Opponents have high trust and low agreement. They trust your competence and capabilities but do not agree with your ideas, decisions, and projects. They will often challenge you, ask questions, and seek clarification.

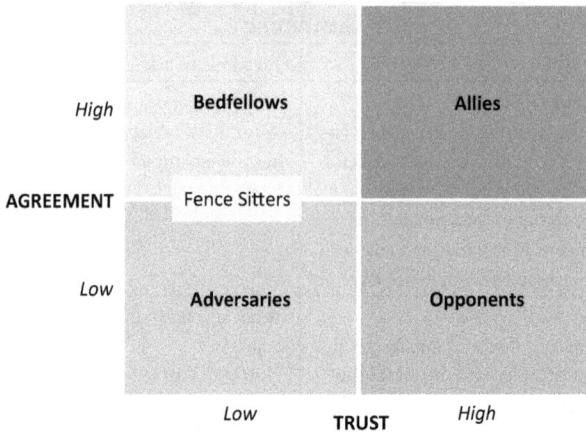

Figure 3.15 Types of stakeholders

Bedfellows have high agreement and low trust. They agree with your
   ideas, decisions, and projects but don't have the trust that you are
   the right person to execute them.

Fence sitters have low trust but neither high nor low agreement. They
   don't trust your competence and capabilities. They will stay neutral—
   neither support nor oppose your ideas, decisions, and projects.

Allies have high trust and high agreement. They trust your competence
   and capabilities and are strong advocates of your ideas, decisions, and
   projects. You can confide in them and ask them for honest feedback.

With empathy, you will be able to influence people better. Once you
understand what people think, feel, and will, it will be easier to influence
them. The first step is to assess your power source and then select an
influencing style.

Following are the sources of power that you might have access to in
your organization:

a. Position power

   It comes from an individual's role and status within an organization. It has to do with their position and often carries with it the
   right to organize people and resources. This power is conferred by
   the organization. So if the job is lost, power is lost too.

b. Sanction power

   It encompasses both rewards and coercion, stemming from the ability to offer incentives or impose threats to influence people's actions.

c. Expert power

It arises from the unique expertise or skills possessed by an individual, which they can choose to share or withhold. Frequently, individuals are willing to be influenced by those they perceive as experts in a particular field.

d. Information power

It comes from the ability to selectively control the flow of information either horizontally or vertically.

e. Network power

It comes from controlling or using access to influential people, networks, or associations.

f. Personal power

It comes from one's ability to be reliable, trustworthy, honest, likeable, and charismatic.

Once the power source is known, you must select a particular influencing style to connect with the person. There are following five main influencing styles:

1. Logic
2. Emotive appeal
3. Leveraging relationship
4. Barter/bargaining
5. Force

The appropriate influencing style depends on various factors such as importance, urgency, complexity, and future relationships. You need to be flexible in using a different influencing style with the same person under different circumstances.

1. Logic

This approach relies on employing logic, facts, and rational data to present your argument. It is effective when dealing with individuals who think logically and sequentially. To succeed, you must provide compelling evidence and refrain from exaggeration, emotional appeals, or unsupported opinions. Your role is to be viewed as an impartial presenter of evidence, leading to a logical conclusion.

2. Emotive appeal

This method taps into individuals' emotions or sentiments, motivating them to act in a particular manner. It might stem from the fear of potential outcomes, a sense of belonging to a group, the exhilaration of success, the determination to uphold personal values, the satisfaction of contributing to a greater cause, a sense of duty towards doing what is right, and so forth.

3. Leveraging relationship

This style involves influencing through the use of existing connections and rapport. The effectiveness of this approach depends on the strength of the relationship; the stronger the bond, the greater the influence.

4. Barter/bargaining

This style involves trading or negotiating—offering something in exchange for another's cooperation. Prior to negotiations, it is advantageous to cultivate a positive perception in other person's mind. This style can be combined with other influencing methods.

5. Force

Though this style is effective for achieving compliance, it seldom garners genuine commitment. This approach typically requires some form of authority or power to enforce compliance. It may be suitable for expediting tasks, but caution is warranted as it often breeds resentment, which may surface later on.

Activity

Step 1: Assess your empathy

Step 2: Collect data about the person/people you want to empathize with

Step 3: Analysis of Think–Feel–Will

Follow the steps 1, 2, and 3 given on pages 81, 82, and 83.

Step 4: Stakeholder Management

Once you do the think–feel–will analysis, you fill in the following sheet on stakeholder management:

Stakeholder management	
To what extent is/are the stakeholder/stakeholders affected?	Type (ally, opponent, adversary, bedfellow, fence sitter)
How critical is their buy-in?	How to deal with this person?

Stakeholder management	
What is the best time to approach?	Is there someone who can help me connect or influence the person?
Is there any additional information required before I meet with the person?	

Step 5: Access your power source

Power source	
How much power can I leverage from my position in the organization?	Can I use any sanction power?
Am I perceived as an expert? Can I leverage my expertise?	Do I have any critical information that others don't have?
Can I leverage any power from my network?	How much of my personal power can I leverage?
What is my best power source?	

Step 6: Select an appropriate influencing style to influence the stakeholder

Fill out the following sheet :

Influencing style	
Context	Factors that will determine my influencing style
The influencing style I will use and why?	
Examples of what I will say/the phrases that I will use.	What specific actions will I take?

3. Networking

Digital leaders need to have a reliable network—or a group of people whom they trust and rely on to get things done. In the Harvard Business Review article, *How leaders create and use networks*, the authors Ibarra and Hunter recommend building three types of networks:

1. Operational—people you need to accomplish your assigned routine tasks
2. Personal—people who can help you with personal achievement
3. Strategic—people outside your control who will enable you to reach key organizational objectives

To succeed, one must develop a strategic network using empathy as it can accelerate your own and your company's growth and performance.

Figure 3.16 shows the six important steps of building a network, which are divided into three phases: identify, contact, and cultivate.

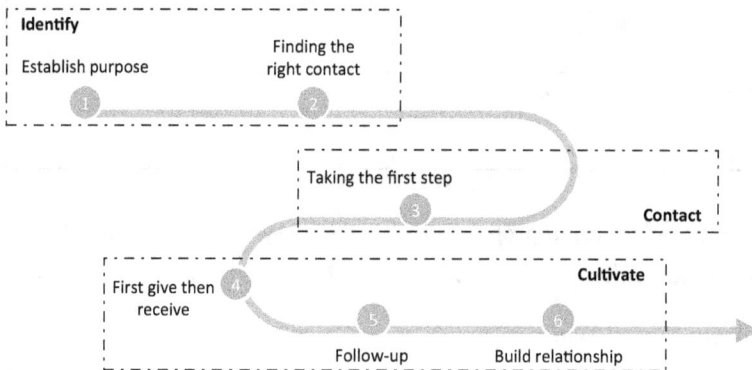

Figure 3.16 Three phases of network building

Identify

1. Establish purpose
   Ask yourself why you want to network with this person. What value will it provide you? What value will it bring to that person? How will your business benefit from it?

2. Find the right contact

   If the person is in your organization, try to seek more information about him/her either from LinkedIn or through your existing network within your organization.

   Contact

3. Take the first step

   It is important that the person with whom you will connect is more informal and open to networking. Unless you take the first step, you won't really understand if he/she is the right person to network. If you meet the person physically, after mutual introductions, you can start the conversation on a common topic, project, or even a person. Be empathetic and use active listening to understand what the person thinks, feels, and wills. Make him/her feel that you are here to help him/her and not seek immediate gain. Add him/her to your online social networks. If you want to connect with a person on social media such as LinkedIn, always write a small note (less than 200 words) when you send him/her a request, explaining how the connection can be mutually beneficial to each other. If you are in the same city, make sure you meet in person. For example, in Sweden, it is a customary practice to network over *fika*: coffee and cookies.

   Cultivate

4. First give then receive

   Always think first about what you can offer to the person rather than what you can receive from him/her. If you are connected on social media, observe the person's behavior. See what type of articles and posts he/she writes. If you genuinely like them, do post your comments or reviews on it. You can also open a discussion on a certain topic.

5. Follow-up

   Following up with the network is the most important step as it helps in nurturing and strengthening it. However, research shows that even though most people agree that networking is essential, less than 50 percent manage to follow up or stay in touch with their network. In total, 41 percent of them said that they would like to interact more, but they have no time.[4] You can follow up in many ways such as emails, newsletters, social media posts, phone calls, video chats, or face-to-face meetings, endorsing their skills on LinkedIn, promoting their services, or referring them to others. Remember to be respectful and professional, respect their time and privacy, and follow up on your promises and commitments.

6. Build relationship

Strive to move from a formal relationship to a more informal one. This would happen when you have developed mutual trust and confidence in each other. At this point, after you have offered enough help, you might seek help or favors from them. Don't expect too much and don't be disappointed if your contact may not be able to help you at present. Normally, most professionals would return the favors you do to them, sooner or later, in some way or the other.

Use the following sheet for networking:

Identify	
Name of the person:	Location:
Why do you want to network? What value will it provide to your business? What value can he/she provide you? What impact will it have on your business?	
Which unit/team is he/she currently working? What were the previous roles? Do you have any common contacts? Is the person located in the same city? How many years of experience he/she has? What is his/her area of expertise? What are his/her hobbies, certifications, and extracurricular activities?	
Contact	
Do you see any common interests? Is there a project that you would like to discuss? Is there a topic other than business you would like to begin conversations on?	

Contact
Do you have a common connection?
Can your common connection introduce you to each other?

Cultivate
What can you offer the person? How can you help the person?
How will you follow up? How frequently will you follow up?
If you meet your contact in person, use the think–feel–will empathy analysis for building relationship. What does the person think about me?
How does the person feel about our connection?
What does the person need from me?
How formal is your relationship? Rate on a scale of 1 to 5, 1: lowest, 5: highest
How can you make it more friendly and informal?

4. Mentoring and Reverse Mentoring

Empathy can be a useful competency in mentoring as well as reverse mentoring. Some companies have a young advisory board comprising a group of talented junior colleagues and millennials, who offer strategic advice to the executives. They need mentoring where a leader can guide and inspire them to plan out their career roadmaps. In return, they can offer reverse mentoring on use cases and practical applications of the latest digital technologies.

A one-day hackathon was organized in a company by the strategy team, where around 50 millennials participated. The topic was how to transition the business to metaverse. They were divided into teams of five, where they were asked to come up with a topic of their choice. Then they had to make a presentation explaining their new ideas before the head of strategy. Some amazing ideas came up. The top three ones were selected and taken to the next level to be further developed and discussed.

I had the privilege to be under the guidance of a mentor during the formative years of my professional career. He taught me a very valuable networking lesson:

> *One must invest time and effort in building relationships and helping people. It will pay back someday for sure.*

To emphasize his point, he shared his story. When he was working with a Nordic multinational company, he was deputed on a long-term assignment to the United States as the head of a customer unit. But before his appointment, he had to clear interviews. First, with the head of the North American market, his hiring manager. Second, with the customer's chief technology officer (CTO). At the interview, the first question the CTO asked him was—how close he was to his company's CEO? If there is an escalation, how fast can they reach the CEO through him?

Mentoring

The following sheet will help you be a better mentor using empathy.

Name of the person you want to mentor:	
What is the value for you? What is the value for the person? How mentoring will help the business? Think–feel–will analysis What does the person think about mentoring? How does the person feel about mentoring? What does the person need from your mentoring?	

Do you have any specific topics you would like to mentor?
What is the timeline?
How would you measure success?

Reverse Mentoring

The following sheet will help you be a better reverse mentor using empathy.

Name of the person you want to reverse mentor:	
What is the value for you? What is the value for the person?	
How reverse mentoring will help the business?	
Think–feel–will analysis	
What does the person think about reverse mentoring?	
How does the person feel about reverse mentoring?	
What does the person need from your reverse mentoring?	
Do you have any specific topics you would like to get reverse mentored on?	
What is the timeline?	
How would you measure success?	

Summary

- Empathy is the ability to understand other people's emotions. It is about understanding what others think, feel, and will (desire).
- There are three distinct types of empathy: cognitive empathy, emotional empathy, and empathic concern.
  - Cognitive empathy is the ability to understand another person's perspective or simply understand what other people think *(Think)*.
  - Emotional empathy is the ability to feel what someone else feels *(Feel)*.
  - Empathic concern is the ability to sense what another person needs from you *(Will)*.
- Based on different motivations, people can be classified into type 1, type 2, type 3, type 4, and type 5.
- The 4D model classifies people as dreamers, designers, doubters, and doers.
- Empathy can be successfully incorporated into team building, stakeholder management and influencing, networking, and mentoring and reverse mentoring.

CHAPTER 4

Competency 3: Informed Decision-Making

As part of its digital transformation program, a retail company in Europe wanted to invest in building a new AI platform to improve its online customer experience. The company had operations in over 25 countries across the globe, with around 500 physical brick-and-mortar outlets. A few years ago, it had launched an online retail platform to offer its customers an omni-channel shopping experience. The traffic on the platform had shown a considerable growth over the years. It was at its peak during the pandemic times. The company wanted to increase sales by offering its customers a better experience. It wanted to build the next version of the online platform based on AI.

Barry Richards (name changed), the head of IT at the retail company, was heading this project. He had a global team of 35 IT professionals. The retail company had outsourced its operations and maintenance to an IT consulting service vendor, who was also responsible for the operations and support of the online platform, along with other tools and software. Barry had a leadership team of five people: Maurice, the director of operations, Sanne, the director of customer support, Sam, the director of cloud and platforms, Nina, the director of security, and Arun, the director of development and testing (all names changed). At the leadership team meeting, Barry announced that the executive management had decided to invest 750k euros into building a new platform based on AI capabilities.

The retail company's relatively small IT team did not have the competence and capabilities to build the platform in-house. They had to find an external vendor. Barry and his team issued a Request for Proposal (RFP), where they listed the following key capabilities for the platform:

- Personalized recommendations
- Tracking the customer behavior

- Business insights
- Data security
- Cloud and data analytics

The platform development project was supposed to have three phases: consulting, build, and integration. In the consulting phase, the vendor would gather all the business requirements in detail from the customer. In the build phase, the vendor would perform the development and testing of the platform. And, in the integration phase, the platform would be introduced in the customer's IT environment and interfaced with other tools and systems. Data and applications would be migrated to it from the old platform.

After all the detailed requirements were listed, RFP was open for the prospective vendors to submit their preliminary proposals. The RFP had three rounds. Round 1 was the initial screening, where five vendors would be shortlisted for the next round. In Round 2, the shortlisted vendors would be invited for an open interview, where they could ask questions or seek clarifications. They would then submit a detailed proposal along with a technical solution and commercials. Out of them, two or a maximum of three vendors, would be selected for the final Round 3. A detailed evaluation and due diligence would be done on the vendors. There would also be another open interview where they could ask further questions on the project requirements and get to know more about the customer. The vendors could revise the proposal if they wanted to. Barry and his team would then select the final vendor to award the AI platform development contract.

The RFP received a good response from the market. Fifteen vendors responded with their preliminary proposals, out of which four were existing ones, and the remaining eleven were new ones. Barry and his team decided to move the four existing ones and the new one to the next round as they did not want to take risks with the ones with whom they did not have a business relationship before. For the final round, there were three vendors: A, B, and C. A was the existing vendor. B was the new vendor. And C was the existing vendor, the same one managing the company's current operations.

Vendor A had its own AI platform. However, it was built and customized for customers in the healthcare industry. It was never sold to any retail customers. The platform had to be fine-tuned and customized as per retail requirements. Vendor A was proposing a team of three consultants, seven developers, one solution architect, and one project manager to deliver the project in six months: one month for consulting, three months for platform customization, and two months for integration and deployment, for a price of 586,400 euros.

Vendor A	Headcounts	Hours	Rate per hour	Subtotal
Consultant	3	160	90	43,200
Developer	7	800	80	448,000
Solution Architect	1	320	110	35,200
Project Manager	1	500	120	60,000
Total				586,400

Vendor B had no platform of its own. However, it had a partnership with a digital startup who had a developed AI platform customized for retail. The platform was sold before by the startup to a retail customer independently and not through a partnership with Vendor B. It was proposing a team of two consultants, five developers, one solution architect, and one project manager to deliver the project in four months: one month for consulting, one month for customization, and two months for integration and deployment, for a price of 777,000 euros.

Vendor B	Headcounts	Hours	Rate per hour	Subtotal
Consultant	2	540	175	189,000
Developer	5	480	150	360,000
Solution Architect	1	480	225	108,000
Project Manager	1	480	250	120,000
Total				777,000

Vendor C had no platform of its own. However, it was willing to invest its own funds into developing the AI platform to strengthen its current business relationship further with the retail company. It was proposing a team of three consultants, seven developers, two solution architects, and one project manager to deliver the project in a year: one month for consulting, six months for development, and five months for integration and deployment, for a price of 413,600 euros.

Vendor C	Headcounts	Hours	Rate per hour	Subtotal
Consultant	3	160	30	14,400
Developer	7	1760	25	308,000
Solution Architect	2	480	45	43,200
Project Manager	1	960	50	48,000
Total				413,600

The open interview was scheduled the following week. The technical and sales team from all the vendors had arrived at Barry's office. Out of the three vendors, Vendor B looked very prepared and was asking many questions. Some of them were quite straightforward and difficult. Barry wanted to see a prototype or a platform demo. The following week, Vendors A and B were invited to the office at different times to showcase their product demos. Vendor C had no prototype to showcase. It would take them at least three weeks to build one. None of the vendors revised their offers after the interview.

It was a difficult decision for Barry and his team to select a vendor. Barry first asked Maurice about his decision. He suggested Vendor C. Although it had a delivery time of one year, it had the lowest price and an existing working relationship. Arun and Nina voted for Vendor A. Its price was within the budget with a reasonable delivery time of six months. Sanne and Sam voted for Vendor B. Though over the budget, it had a ready custom-made niche partner product with a good reference or testimonial from other retail customer. It had the shortest delivery time of four months. Barry had to make the final decision in the next two weeks. But before, he wanted to see the demo from Vendor C. So he postponed his final decision by another week. After three weeks of anticipated wait time, Barry awarded the contract to Vendor C. His decision was appreciated by the executives and the CEO but surprised most of his leadership team.

After a year, Barry realized that he made a wrong decision. Vendor C had insufficient AI competence, could not cope up with timelines, and ran out of development funds. Where did Barry go wrong? Instead of an informed decision he made a biased decision. He made decision based on his gut feeling instead of data.

Informed decision-making involves making decisions based on accurate, reliable, and relevant information. It involves gathering and analyzing data, considering multiple perspectives, and using critical thinking skills to evaluate options and make the best choice.[1]

However, most of the business decisions are made by gut feelings or emotions, without giving much consideration to the factual data. As per an article in Harvard Business Review, *The Hidden Traps in Decision Making*, there are six hidden traps in decision-making that enable one to make a biased decision:

1. Anchoring trap
2. Status quo trap
3. Sunk cost trap
4. Confirming evidence trap
5. Framing trap
6. Estimates and forecast trap

As per human psychology, *anchoring* trap is a cognitive bias that describes the common human tendency to rely too heavily on the first piece of information offered (the *anchor*) when making decisions.[2] At a workshop, while I was explaining the concept of anchor trap to my team, I conducted an experiment where people were divided into two groups. One group was asked to answer the following two questions:

- Is the population of Mumbai greater than 20 million?
- What is your best estimate of Mumbai's population?

The other group was asked:

- Is the population of Mumbai greater than 60 million?
- What is your best estimate of Mumbai's population?

It was observed that the difference in answers to the second question for both groups was large. The figure cited in the first question influenced the answer to the second question due to the anchoring effect.

Barry became a victim of the anchor trap. The first piece of information he received was from Maurice, who opted for Vendor C. He also knew Maurice personally and professionally for over 10 years, better than other team members. Hence, his decision was weighted disproportionately compared to others.

In the *status quo* trap, there is a tendency to maintain things as they are, even if they may seem significantly less optimal. The source of the status quo trap lies deep within our psyche. A study was conducted where a group of professionals who were in the jobs at their respective firms for more than a decade were asked the reason for staying so long and not switching to better opportunities. Most of them replied that it was due to fear of moving away from the status quo. Breaking the status quo demands taking some action. When we act, we take responsibility. When things go well, we get the credit. And when things go wrong, we get criticism and blame. In most cases, a person would prefer to stick to the status quo as it is the safer course putting one at less psychological risk. In business, where sins of commission (doing something) tend to be punished more severely than sins of omission (doing nothing), people prefer the status quo. For example, in a situation where a company is undergoing a reorganization, where things are uncertain, most of the good decisions that can positively impact the business are put on hold.

Barry fell into the status quo trap too. The IT operations were well managed by Vendor C. Barry being a risk-averse, did not want to experiment with a new Vendor B and did not want to proceed with a more expensive Vendor A than C.

The *sunk cost* trap comes from our innate tendency to make current decisions based on the decisions made in the past that hold no relevance in the present. Our decisions of the past which are termed as *sunk costs* can be the old investments of time and money that are now irrecoverable and irrelevant to our present decision. It is difficult for most people to overcome this trap because they are reluctant to admit the mistakes they made in the past. They continue to justify their past decision with the fear of how they would look in public or what would people think of them when their mistakes are exposed. For example, if a manager hires a person and the person does not perform as per the expectations, instead of letting him go, the manager will normally tend to keep him longer as firing the person would publicly expose his poor hiring choice.

The *confirming evidence* trap comes from the tendency to give too much weight to the evidence that supports a view we already have and not enough weight to contradictory evidence. It is because we tend to subconsciously decide what we want to do before we figure out why we want to do it. Also, we tend to be more inclined and drawn by things we like than the things we dislike. Imagine you are the hiring manager and want to hire a software developer with experience in python to develop an AI application. You interview the person and are impressed by his personality. However, the person does not have any experience with python programming. Other candidates have better experience than him. But you like the person's attitude toward learning and have decided to hire him. You talk to your first team lead who interviewed him. He tells you not to hire him as he does not have the kind of experience your team is looking for. You get a conflicting viewpoint. Then you talk to your second team lead who also interviewed him. He tells you that even though the person lacks experience with python, he demonstrates a strong potential to learn. He will be able to pick up fast if we provide him with adequate training. This confirms your viewpoint, and you finalize him for the position.

Barry fell into the confirming evidence trap. He already had made up his mind to award the contract to Vendor C. The feedback he received from Maurice and the successful demo of the prototype showcased by Vendor C in three weeks supported his viewpoint.

The *framing* trap is about individuals making decisions based on how an issue is presented or *framed*, rather than the facts presented. People in most cases choose an option that maximizes the prospect of a positive outcome while avoiding responses that entail a risk of loss.[3] There was a classic experiment conducted by the decision-making researchers, Daniel Kahneman and Amos Tversky. They posed the following problem to a group of insurance professionals:

You are a marine property adjuster charged with minimizing the loss of cargo on three insured barges that sank yesterday off the coast of Alaska. Each barge holds U.S.$200,000 worth of cargo, which will be lost if not salvaged within 72 hours. The owner of a local marine salvage company gives you two options, both of which will cost the same:

Option A: This option will save the cargo of one of the three barges, worth U.S.$200,000.

Option B: This option has a one-third probability of saving the cargo on all three barges, worth U.S.$600,000, but has a two-thirds probability of saving nothing.

It was observed that 71 percent of the respondents chose the less risky Option A, which will save one barge for sure. Another group in the study was asked to choose between Options C and D.

Option C: This plan will result in the loss of two of the three cargoes, worth U.S.$400,000.

Option D: This plan has a two-thirds probability of resulting in the loss of all three cargoes, the entire U.S.$600,000, but has a one-third probability of losing no cargo.

It was observed that 80 percent of these respondents preferred Option D.

Option A is the same as Option C, and Option B is the same as Option D. However, they are framed in different ways. The different responses reveal that the fear of loss is greater than the prospects of winning, even though the odds may be identical.[4]

In the *estimating and forecasting* trap, people get too locked into their original estimations and forecasts and are unwilling to change when new information becomes available. This trap is described in three distinct types: the overconfidence trap, the prudence trap, and the recallability trap.[5] The *overconfidence* trap occurs when people become overconfident that their decisions will be accurate. This can lead to errors in judgment and in turn bad decisions. The *prudence* trap occurs when a group decides to play it safe rather than lose big on a high-risk option. When faced with high-stake decisions, they tend to adjust their estimates or forecasts just to be on the safe side. The *recallability* trap occurs when a group fails to accurately forecast the future based on its knowledge of the past.

As it frequently bases its predictions about future events on its memory of past events, it can be overly influenced by dramatic events—those that leave a strong impression on its memory.

Informed decision-making is important for a digital leader because:

- Informed decisions based on careful analysis of relevant data and information reduce the risk of making poor or ill-informed choices that can harm the team.
- Decisions based on accurate and relevant information are more likely to lead to positive outcomes such as increased profitability, productivity, and customer satisfaction.
- Informed decision-making based on sound judgment and careful consideration can improve the credibility of managers and the team they lead.
- When managers involve team members in the decision-making process and consider their concerns and feedback, it can build trust and foster a sense of shared ownership in the organization.
- Informed decision-making can promote innovation and creativity as managers can better identify new opportunities and take calculated risks to drive growth and success.

Informed decision-making involves making a complete decision using three levers:

- Rational
- Emotional
- Instinctual

A study shows that most leaders make decisions based on either one of the above levers. Most of the decisions are made rationally or instinctually. Very few are made emotionally. In a survey by McKinsey, only 20 percent of the respondents said their organizations excel at decision-making,[6] while a majority of them said that much of the time they devote to decision-making is used ineffectively.

All three levers leverage data.

Rational   **Emotional**   **Instinctual**

Figure 4.1 *Three levers of informed decision-making*

Rational involves using data based on facts, figures, surveys, and statistics, which are generated from business operations.

Emotional involves using people data generated from daily interactions with people such as team members and stakeholders.

Instinctual involves using data based on risks, probability, opinions, and inputs from stakeholders, which are generated from the experience of the decision makers.

Rational decisions only can be risky. They may miss opportunities or overlook threats, and may not consider the needs of the stakeholders/employees. Emotional decisions only could be illogical and risky. They might help one win the support of people but may not be the best for achieving business goals and objectives. Instinctual decisions only could be reflexive or impulsive without considering the underlying facts and emotions of people. Thus, informed decision-making should be rational, emotional, and instinctual.

Figure 4.2 shows the informed decision-making model based on three levers: rational, emotional, and instinctual. It comprises three phases: Define, Act, and Review.

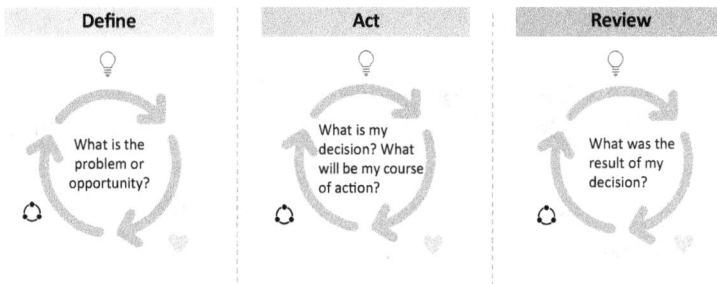

Define

What is the problem or opportunity?

Act

What is my decision? What will be my course of action?

Review

What was the result of my decision?

Figure 4.2 *Informed decision-making model*

In the *Define* phase, you define the issue/problem to be resolved or an opportunity to be explored. In the *Act* phase, you plan out the course of action and then execute the decision. In the *Review* phase, you analyze the outcome.

Activity

Use the following sheet for informed decision-making in case of a problem to be resolved.

Define
What is the problem to be resolved?
Rational: What are the costs incurred in solving the problem? How much is the expected lead time? Is this problem generic or specific? Are there any facts, figures, or statistics available to support decision-making? Emotional: Who are the stakeholders involved? What is their position? What is their level of knowledge and expertise? Do we need to involve additional resources? Instinctual: What is the current situation? Are there any risks involved? Do we have experience of dealing with similar problems in the past? What is our gut feeling?
Act
What is our decision? Why did we make this decision?
Rational: What actions will we take to solve the problem? Do we have a strategy? What are the costs involved? Do we have a detailed plan of action?

(Continued)

(*Continued*)

Act
Emotional: Do we have enough resources? What are their expertise? How will we communicate with them? How will we ensure they remain motivated? Instinctual: Do we have a positive feeling about our decision? Does it align with our personal values? Does it align with the business ethics and values? Are we aware of the risks?

Review
What was the result of our decision?
Rational: Was the rational data helpful in decision-making? Did we manage to deliver within cost limits? Did we meet the deadlines? Did we meet the customer expectations? Emotional: Was the emotional data helpful in decision-making? Did the stakeholder/employees remain motivated? Were their needs met? Do they feel their efforts were worthwhile? Instinctual: Was the instinctual data helpful in decision-making? What could have been done better? How would you reuse this experience in future decision-making? Were we able to manage risks?

Use the following sheet for informed decision-making in case of an opportunity to be explored.

Define
What is the opportunity to be explored?
Rational: How much will be the revenue increase? How much will be the cost reduction? Will it improve the customer experience? Are there any facts, figures, or statistics available to support decision-making?

Define
Emotional: Who are the stakeholders involved? What is their position? What is their level of knowledge and expertise? Do we need to involve additional resources? Instinctual: What is the current situation? Are there any risks involved? Have we explored similar opportunities in the past? What is our gut feeling?

Act
What is our decision? Why did we make this decision?
Rational: What actions will we take to explore the opportunity? Do we have a strategy? What are the costs involved? Do we have a detailed plan of action? Emotional: Do we have enough resources? What are their expertise? How will we communicate with them? How will we ensure they remain motivated? Instinctual: Do we have a positive feeling about our decision? Does it align with our personal values? Does it align with the business ethics and values? Are we aware of the risks?

Review
What was the result of our decision?
Rational: Was the rational data helpful in decision-making? Is the revenue improved? Are the costs reduced? Are the customer expectations met?

(*Continued*)

(*Continued*)

Review
Emotional: Was the emotional data helpful in decision-making? Did the stakeholder/employees remain motivated? Were their needs met? Do they feel their efforts were worthwhile? Instinctual: Was the instinctual data helpful in decision-making? What could have been done better? How would we reuse this experience in future decision-making? Were we able to manage risks?

Summary

- Informed decision-making involves making decisions based on accurate, reliable, and relevant information. It involves gathering and analyzing data, considering multiple perspectives, and using critical thinking skills to evaluate options and make the best choice.
- There are six hidden traps in decision-making that enable one to make a biased decision: anchoring trap, status quo trap, sunk cost trap, confirming evidence trap, framing trap, estimates and forecast trap.
- Informed decision-making involves making a complete decision using three levers: rational, emotional, and instinctual.
- Rational involves using data based on facts, figures, surveys, and statistics, which are generated from business operations.
- Emotional involves using people data generated from daily interactions with people such as team members and stakeholders.
- Instinctual involves using data based on risks, probability, opinions, and inputs from stakeholders, which are generated from the experience of the decision makers.
- Informed decision-making model comprises three phases: Define, Act, and Review.

CHAPTER 5

Competency 4: Fast Execution

Jessica Carlson (name changed) was newly appointed as the head of digital transformation at a real estate company based in the Nordics. It had a portfolio of over 600 commercial properties and a workforce of around 500 people. The company was recovering from the pandemic downturn in the real estate industry. To grow the business further and make it sustainable in the long run, the executives wanted to make the company *look digital*. To enable transformation across the company, the leadership team created a digital transformation unit under business operations, which was headed by Marianne Nordfeldt (name changed).

Jessica, who had previous experience as a digital transformation program manager at a global retail company, was very excited about the role and had an ambition to develop new ways of working for the business using the latest digital transformation technologies. She started by interviewing different people in different areas to understand the business and the challenges faced by employees and customers. She observed that data, a valuable resource for the business, was fragmented, siloed, and not easily accessible. The company needed a data analytics platform that could help them make better decisions about how to price their properties, identify market trends, and understand customer needs.

Jessica prepared an executive presentation and a business case where she proposed investing in a data analytics platform. She surveyed the data analytics market, conducted due diligence on the vendors, took opinions from the experts, and finally proposed Tableau as the preferred vendor. Tableau is a data analytics software that is widely used in business intelligence. It helps users to see and understand data with its built-in visual best practices. Tableau is also known for its scalability and efficiency, which makes it a popular choice for businesses of all sizes. It gives two hosting options: host on your own server if you have the IT resources to do so or host with Tableau online.

Jessica's proposal was discussed at the final quarterly review meeting of the year by the executive team. It was December. Holidays were around the corner. The executive team had many other pending priorities and actions to close before the end of the year and was reluctant to start something new. They decided to take some actions in January after they were back from vacation.

Three weeks of the new year passed before people were back from vacation, and the first meeting of the leadership team took place in the last week of January. There were some urgent and pressing matters regarding the commercial properties that needed to be addressed by them. The data analytics proposal was not even there on the meeting agenda.

In the first week of February, Jessica asked Marianne about the status of her proposal. To her surprise, she got feedback that it was not a part of the leadership discussions yet. But Marianne assured her that she would push it as one of the agenda items at the next leadership meeting at the end of February. At the meeting in February, Marianne brought up the proposal before the team. Most of the executives found the Tableau price too expensive. She was asked to renegotiate the offer with them and come up with a better option. If not, then look for some other reliable vendor offering a good price. Jessica came up with a couple more vendors: RapidMiner and Alteryx. The vendor had to be approved by Marianne first and then a final approval would be given by the executive team. But Marianne got tied up with resolving escalations for the recently acquired properties in Norway and Iceland. She was super busy with all-day-long meetings. The decision on the vendor selection stayed pending for six weeks until mid-April, until the escalations were eased off a bit. Marianne then took a week's vacation to recuperate from her burnout.

After she returned, she asked Jessica to invite the vendors to present a product demo in the second week of May. The head of IT and a few technical experts were invited to the meeting. There were a couple of follow-up meetings and workshops that involved heavy technical discussions. There was resistance from the internal IT team to acquire this new platform. The IT team had fewer resources and was very busy managing the daily business operations. They did not want the extra responsibility of new platform management. After much debate and discussion, in the last week of June, Marianne chose Alteryx as the vendor for the data analytics platform.

Then came July, the month of peak summer. In Europe, particularly in the Nordics, it is a common practice to take vacations in July. Both customers and vendors take a break, and the businesses slow down. In the first week of August, Jessica and Marianne met with the IT team to work on a plan of action to be approved by the executives. But as luck would have it, the real estate market went bearish. There was severe budget pressure on the management to cut down costs. The data analytics platform project was put on hold till November. The executives demanded a revision of the budget for the project and resubmit the plan. The plan was resubmitted in December's first week. Again, holidays were around the corner. The approval was pushed to next January. After a yearlong wait, Jessica was frustrated. She resigned a week before Christmas.

What the real estate company's executives lacked was fast execution. They were so tied up with the daily operational tasks that the data analytics platform project kept on getting a lower priority. There was too much planning but no action. You can have the best plan, best team, and best product but unless you take action, nothing happens.

Fast execution is the ability of a leader to take rapid actions in both predictable and unpredictable environments.

A survey was conducted with business leaders to test the gap between decisions and actions under predictable and unpredictable environments. It was observed that in predictable environments:

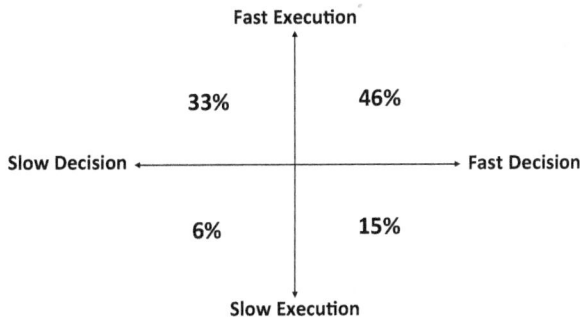

Figure 5.1 Execution-decision matrix in predictable environments

- 46 percent made fast decisions and executed them fast.
- 33 percent made slow decisions but executed them fast.

- 15 percent made fast decisions but executed them slowly.
- 6 percent made slow decisions and executed them slowly.

The combined percentage of fast execution after the decision was 79.

In unpredictable environments:

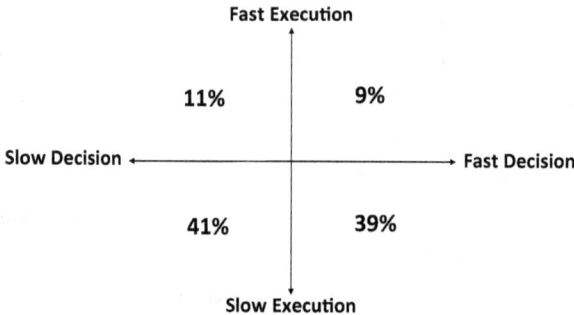

Figure 5.2 Execution-decision matrix in unpredictable environments

- 9 percent made fast decisions and executed them fast.
- 11 percent made slow decisions but executed them fast.
- 39 percent made fast decisions but executed them slowly.
- 41 percent made slow decisions and executed them slowly.

The combined percentage of fast execution after a decision was only 20.

Figure 5.3 shows the predictability continuum. On the left extreme, there is certainty with 100 percent predictability, and the right extreme is uncertainty with 0 percent predictability.

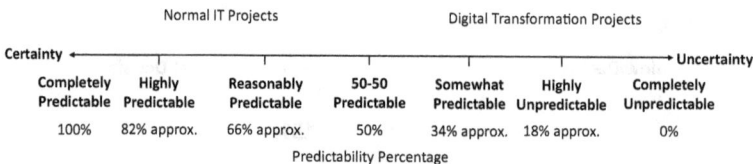

Figure 5.3 Uncertainty continuum

As one moves from left to right, the predictability percentage reduces. Normal IT projects lie on the left side of the continuum, whereas most digital transformation projects lie on the right side.

In predictable environments, there are higher levels of competence, confidence, and credibility among the team.

Competence is the skill required to do a task.
Confidence is the belief that I can do it.
Credibility means I have done it before.

In unpredictable environments, the competence, confidence, and credibility levels among people drop down. A survey was conducted with 51 managers who had experience in driving both normal IT and digital transformation projects. They were asked to rate on a scale of 1 to 10 (1: lowest, 10: highest) for these parameters. Figure 5.4 shows the following rating:

Rating (1: lowest, 10: highest)

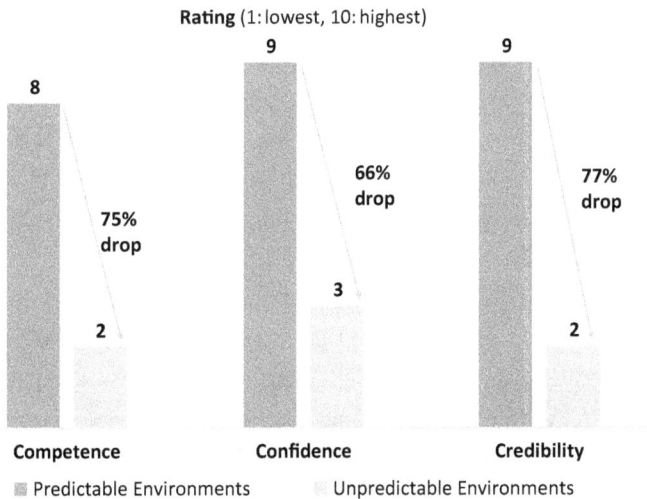

Figure 5.4 Comparison between predictable and unpredictable environments

- Competence showed a 75 percent drop.
- Confidence showed a 66 percent drop.
- Credibility showed a 77 percent drop.

It is because, as discussed earlier, people are more comfortable and trained to handle predictable performances and outcomes than unpredictable ones, which is the cause of failure of most digital transformation projects.

In March 2017, Maersk and IBM announced that they planned to create a global trade digitalization (GTD) platform called TradeLens, for the shipping industry, using blockchain technology. The shipping industry had many challenges. First, most of the processes were manual, error-prone, and involved intense paperwork, which caused the wastage of large amount of resources. The cost of documentation and paperwork was as high as 20 percent of the overall cost of physical transportation. Second was the maritime fraud, which was worth billions of U.S. dollars a year. Third, there was a lack of consistency and availability of information at the origin and destination. Fourth, lack of transparency in the customs process. One could track when the shipment arrived at the port. But one could not predict the expected time to clear the customs.

TradeLens aspired to solve the above problems by providing organizations with a secure digital solution for exchanging digital documents and visibility into the supply chain through commercial solutions such as paperless trade and shipping information pipeline respectively. It would need all the stakeholders in the ecosystem such as freight forwarders, ports, shippers, customs authorities, and even competitors to join, though the value propositions would be different for different players. The major challenge was to sign up a huge network of ecosystem players from 130 operating countries on the platform. It would take at least two to three years to onboard the critical mass. It was important to sign up all the players in the value chain so that it remains smooth and continuous. Any gap caused due to a missing player would result in inefficiencies in the system. Another major challenge was to convince Maersk competitors to join as they would be concerned about sharing their private and confidential data on the platform driven by Maersk, which is one of the big players in the shipping industry.

These challenges continued to persist until the fourth quarter of 2022. Finally, Maersk and IBM made a public announcement in November 2022 to discontinue TradeLens. Rotem Hershko, Head of Business Platforms at A.P Moller-Maersk, said:

TradeLens was founded on the bold vision to make a leap in global supply chain digitization as an open and neutral industry platform. Unfortunately, while we successfully developed a viable platform, the need for full global industry collaboration has not been achieved. As a result, TradeLens has not reached the level of commercial viability necessary to continue work and meet the financial expectations as an independent business. We are deeply grateful for the relentless efforts of our committed industry members and many tech talents, who together have worked diligently to advance the digitalization of the industry through the TradeLens platform. We will leverage the work of TradeLens as a stepping stone to further push our digitization agenda and look forward to harnessing the energy and ability of our technology talent in new ways.[1]

The risks and uncertainty were very high in this digital transformation project. But what we can appreciate is that the leaders at Maersk and IBM took fast action, saw the shortcomings, realized it was not going to work, and quickly terminated the project.

In the book *Just Start*, the authors Schlesinger, Kiefer, and Brown have stated 13 reasons why action trumps everything when the future is unpredictable:

1. If you act, you will find out what works.
2. ...and what doesn't.
3. If you never act, you will never know what is possible and what is not.
4. If you act, you will find out if you like it.
5. ...or you don't.
6. Action leads to a market reaction, which could point you in another direction.
7. As you act, you can find people to come along with you.
8. As you act, you can find ways to do things faster, cheaper, and better.
9. If you act, you won't spend the rest of your life going, "I wondered what would have happened if ..."
10. If all you do is think, you may end up being less interesting as a person.
11. If all you ever do is think about stuff, you can gain tons of theoretical knowledge, but none from the real world.

12. Action always leads to evidence. "Evidence is better than anyone's intuition"—Scott Cook, the founder of Intuit.
13. If you act, you know what is real.

Also, the authors have stated the creaction model: How to act in uncertainty, based on research work by Saras D. Sarasvathy, a professor at the University of Virginia's Darden School of Business. 'Cre'-'action' is based on acting and creating evidence, as contrast to thinking and analysis. Say, you want to start a business. If all you do is think and analyze, you just end up thinking about starting a business. Thinking is a part of creating but without action, nothing is created. You need to take action and collect evidence on what works and what doesn't work. Hence, it is creaction. It complements prediction when things are almost certain.

As per the creaction theory, in the face of uncertainty, use the *act–learn–build* model.

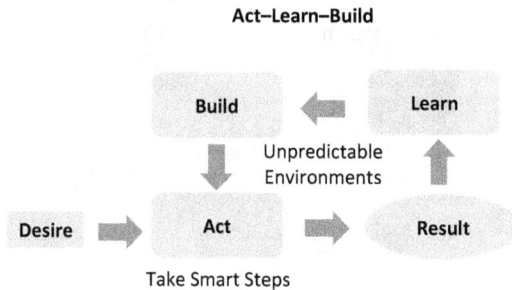

Figure 5.5 The act–learn–build model

More specifically:

1. Take a small, smart step forward.
2. Pause to see what you learn.
3. Build that learning into what to do next.

Smart step is the fast action you take based on:

- Resources at hand within some acceptable limits.
- Your acceptable loss—how much can you afford to lose?

- Bringing in other people—you may choose to bring or not bring them along.
- Your lessons learned and experience built from your last action.

You repeat act–learn–build until one of the following happens:

1. You succeed.
2. No longer want to continue (you change your mind as something else is more appealing).
3. You exceed your acceptable loss.
4. You prove to yourself it can't be done.

To begin an action, you need a desire to do it. It doesn't have to be a strong passion but a sufficient one to get you started.

Taking inspiration from the creaction theory, I would suggest that in the face of certainty, use the *build–act–learn* model.

Build–Act–Learn

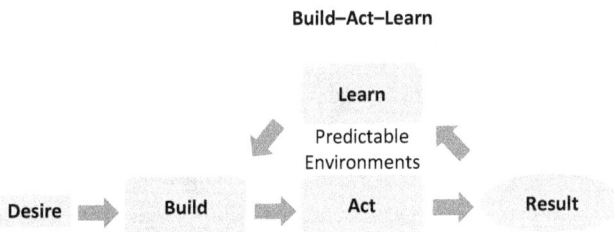

Figure 5.6 The build–act–learn model

More specifically:

1. Build a plan.
2. Act as per the plan.
3. Learn from your actions.

- Planning involves scope of work, timelines, resources, escalation matrix, responsibility matrix, budget estimation, phases, and metrics.
- Act toward achieving your targets.
- Review the project progress at the weekly governance meetings, resolve the issues, share key learnings with the team, and move toward achieving your target.

You repeat build–act–learn until one of the following happens:

- You reach the end of a phase.
- You reach the end of a project.
- Your project is called off.

Regardless of the environment, digital leaders must practice fast execution.

Empowering People

A leader can either fast execute himself/herself or empower people to take quick actions.

A few months ago, I met an ex-colleague of mine. I asked him how he was doing at his new job. He said it was a month since he was driving a workstream in his project, leading a team of four. He only had two major interactions with his manager—on the first day of his project when he was onboarded by him and introduced to the team and customers. And second, when he had a one-to-one meeting with him, the last week. His earlier managers had more of a micromanagement style and were more demanding. So, my ex-colleague found it a bit challenging to adapt to his new manager's working style. He used to ping him for trivial approvals. At the meeting, his new manager clarified his expectations and empowered him to drive the project with autonomy as long as he delivers and gets results. He assured his availability to support him in case of major escalations. But he need not bother him to seek his approvals to run daily operational tasks.

Figure 5.7 shows the various levels of empowerment from E1 to E5.

E1

At this level, leader delegates the task to a team member, tells him/her exactly what to do, and does not involve him/her in the decision-making. The team member may be a fresh graduate or an experienced new hire. The percentage of empowerment is zero.

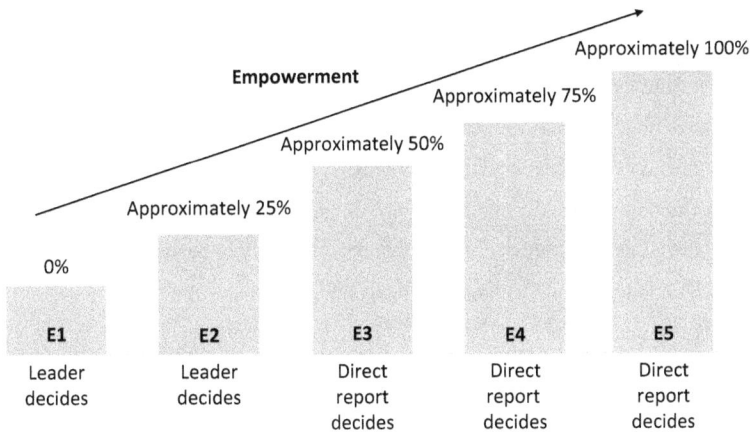

Figure 5.7 Empowerment

E2

At this level, leader delegates the task to a team member, asks him/her what he/she would like to do, and involves him/her to a smaller extent in the decision-making. The final decision is made by the leader. The empowerment is approximately 25 percent.

E3

At this level, leader delegates the task to a team member, asks him/her what he/she would like to do, and involves him/her to a larger extent in the decision-making. The final decision is made by the team member with the approval from the leader. The empowerment is approximately 50 percent.

E4

At this level, leader delegates the task to a team member, does not ask the team member what he/she would like to do, provides full decision-making responsibility to him/her, and does not get involved in the process. The final decision is made by the team member with approval from the leader. The empowerment is approximately 75 percent.

E5

This is the level of absolute empowerment. The leader does not delegate any task. The team member initiates one, with or without the approval from the leader. Full decision-making responsibility is provided to the team member, and the leader does not get involved in the process. The final decision is made by the team member, with or without approval from the leader. The empowerment is 100 percent.

Fast Execution Stories

In 2013, I was deployed on a short term assignment (STA) as an account manager for a customer account in the United States. Nishant Batra, currently the chief strategy and technology officer at Nokia, was the key account manager (KAM) who hired me for the role. I had no previous experience in sales. I was expecting that in the first few weeks, I would interact more with the internal team, get familiar with the new work culture, understand the sales process, and then I would be ready to engage with the customer. But I had a pleasant surprise. On day one, Nishant teamed me up with Chad Wheaton, a sales director on his team. I was asked to work closely with him. He instructed Chad to involve me as much as possible in the customer meetings and help me get up to speed as fast as possible. At around 3 pm on my first day, Chad told me that we were meeting the customer in the evening, not at their office, but at the American Airlines center in Dallas to watch a basketball game—Dallas Mavericks play against Houston Rockets. It was my first experience meeting the customer, and I was meeting them at a place I never imagined. Everyone was enjoying the game. No one was in the mood to talk about business. Dallas Mavs won! The customers were Mavs fans. They were very happy and wanted to celebrate. After the game, we all had dinner at the center. It was quite an eventful evening.

Later in that week, I visited the customer again, but this time at their office. I was well greeted by them. We started our conversation over the basketball game we watched. Chad introduced me to them and made them aware of my role in the team. Then from the second week onward, I was given the responsibility of managing the business as usual and a target of bringing in new sales. I was able to establish a fast way of working with the customer. I replied to their requests with a quotation promptly. The customer was also fast in issuing a purchase order (PO). If there was a delay in releasing the PO from their end, a gentle reminder e-mail would suffice. The basketball game gave me a head-start on building relationships, which was crucial in getting things done faster. Moreover, it began in a friendly and informal setting. Chad also introduced me to the internal stakeholders in my first week. Whenever there were any resistances or bottlenecks with them, I brought it up to Chad immediately. He was very quick and supportive in resolving them.

In the third week, I was given new sales targets: orders booked, net sales realized, and work-in-progress (WIP) cleared, which are common across most organizations. Unless the customer issues a PO, a sale cannot be considered as an order booked. Once the delivery begins, the sales status changes from order booked to WIP. Once the last vendor obligation is complete or an acceptance is received from the customer, whichever first, the sales status changes from WIP to net sales realized.

There was a huge backlog of WIP, which was not progressing due to some issues and escalations. Due to this, there were chances of missing our quarterly net sales targets. We had to act fast. Nishant called in for a meeting with his team, where we planned how to clear the WIP. I had a workshop with the delivery team to understand more about the ground-level issues and what support they need from sales. I immediately scheduled a meeting of sales and delivery team leads with the customer, where we deep-dived into the issues that hindered the progress. We both agreed on a plan of action. It was followed rigorously over three to four weeks. As a result, 65 percent of the pending WIP was realized into net sales. We managed to meet our net sales target.

That year, Nishant's team achieved double the annual targets given to them. I received the salesperson of the quarter recognition. Nishant and Chad received the Annual Sales Excellence awards. Everyone on the team was motivated and energetic. It was a high-performing team. It was because of Nishant's belief and demonstration of fast execution through empowerment.

———————————

Recently, when I was flying to London from Istanbul, a Turkish gentleman happened to be in my next seat. We began conversing. Soon we discovered many things in common—we both love London, we both work in IT, and we both have a common professional contact. The gentleman's name was Alisan Erdemli. His purpose to visit London was to meet his business partner in Cambridge. I was amazed to learn that Alisan has been a serial entrepreneur for the past 20 years and was curious to know what motivated him to persevere for so long. I had all the time to hear his story on my four-hour-long flight.

After graduating from Ege University in 2002 with a degree in computer engineering, Alisan started his career with a software consulting firm based out of Istanbul, where he worked with clients mainly from the finance and telecom industry. After working for five years, he felt it was time to start his own venture as there was a lot of demand for IT services in the market, which was picking up after the dot.com bubble burst. Alisan with his brother, also a software engineer based in London, bootstrapped a company named Gobito Enterprise Solutions in the United Kingdom. The firm's objective was to create new bespoke products and deliver projects for customers. The first product was public key infrastructure (PKI) based on digital security which took two years to develop. The purpose of a PKI is to facilitate the secured electronic transfer of information for a range of network activities such as e-commerce, Internet banking, and confidential e-mail. It is required for activities where simple passwords are an inadequate authentication method; more rigorous proof is required to confirm the identity of the parties involved in the communication and to validate the information being transferred.[2] The first major decision Gobito had to make was where to sell the product—the United Kingdom or Turkey? It was decided to sell it in Turkey. So, in 2008, the Gobito branch in Turkey was established. Being a startup, it was very difficult to secure trust from the customers. They lost the competition to an incumbent American multinational financial services company. Gobito sold the product at a reasonable price to a private company that partnered closely with the Turkish government and exited the market.

Alison and his brother had to make a second major decision—to continue with the venture or go back to salaried jobs. They decided to continue. They began developing a new product—automated e-mails. To keep the cash flowing, they acquired two bespoke product development contracts: e-commerce and CRM, from different customers. Both brothers worked for long hours. In 2009, they decided to sell their automated e-mails product under the brand name *Client Grow*. In 2010, after struggling for months, they managed to acquire 10 customers. After delivering the e-commerce product to the customer in 2010, they launched an e-commerce platform under the brand *just4fivepounds* in the United Kingdom to capitalize upon the great market opportunity. They onboarded new partners in the United Kingdom to run the brand.

Soon, Client Grow was outsmarted by the competition, a large-sized IT firm that offered a similar product with a one-year free trial. It was unable to match the competition's offering. Moreover, it also began losing its acquired customer base to them, one by one. It was decided to phase out Client Grow in 2012. The same year its CRM product was phased out too. The only one to continue was just4fivepounds. It was a wholesaler platform supplying products in bulk to retail stores. It began to grow steadily for three consecutive years. However, the partners were incapable of running the business. They made some wrong decisions due to which just4fivepounds incurred heavy losses. Finally, they had to shut down the brand in 2014.

In 2012, Alison was hired by a telecom company as a contractor to manage the development process of a learning management system (LMS) product by a third party. After version 1.0 was developed, the company gave the contract to Gobito to develop version 2.0 of the LMS. The project was completed in 2015. In 2016, the company's CEO wanted to develop a learning platform for the general public. The contract was given again to Gobito, where they would retain the rights to the source code and the telecom company would sell the product to enterprises as value-added services (VAS). However, after a while, the situation changed and the telecom company wanted full ownership, which it acquired from Gobito for U.S.$1 million.

Alison and his brother saw the market opportunity offered by the LMS platform and invested the millions earned through the telecom company deal into developing a new brand Akademi.net. It has two main offerings: Akademi.net LMS and Akademi.net massive open online courses (MOOC). Akademi.net LMS is next-gen customizable learning management system designed for enterprise use to meet its educational development and learning needs. Akademi.net MOOC helps learners meet their educational development and learning needs through thousands of online courses. Instructors can publish their courses on the MOOC platform as well.[3]

Soon, Akademi.net had a competitor that started offering an LMS platform for free and charged customers for the content. They started losing customers to the competition as Akademi.net could not afford to offer the platform for free. To differentiate its content, Alison created a new brand called Cinema8, which allows users to create interactive video experiences through drag-and-drop tools such as questions, feedback buttons, custom forms, clickable areas, and more. To support the easy creation of e-learning content, a new product known as *wowslides* was developed, which allows customers to convert PowerPoint presentations into web content. Today, Akademi.net has three million subscribers, and Cinema8 has 100+ enterprise customers.

I was amazed to hear his story. There was so much unpredictability, risks, and uncertainty. But Alison and his brother moved fast to fail fast and learn fast. His 20 years of serial entrepreneurial experience taught him the following:

1. Focus on one venture at a time.
2. Leverage venture capitalist funding if available.
3. Hire sales and marketing experts who can take your business to the next level.
4. If you can pivot your business well, nothing can stop you from chasing your dreams.

Cultivating Fast Execution

Follow the seven steps below to cultivate fast execution in an unpredictable environment:

Step 1: List top 3 actions

Prepare a list of up to three actions that you would take next. Rate on a scale of 1 to 5, how strong is your desire to take these actions. 1: lowest, 5: highest.

1: very low desire, 2: low desire, 3: moderate desire, 4: high desire, 5: very high desire

Actions	Desire rating (scale of 1 to 5)
1.	
2.	
3.	

The following questions can help you with the preceding list of three actions:

- Why do I want to take this action?
- How important and urgent it is to take this action?
- When should I act?
- What exactly should I do?
- Have I done this before?

Step 2: Desire rating and acceptable loss

Next is to determine an acceptable loss. It can be in terms of money, time, professional reputation, personal reputation, missed opportunities, or other.

In the following sheet, write acceptable loss next to each action:

- What will I lose?
- How much can I afford to lose?
- How much am I willing to lose?

Provide an affordability rating for each action on a scale of 1 to 5, 1: lowest and 5: highest, 1: very low affordability, 2: low affordability, 3: moderate affordability, 4: high affordability, 5: very high affordability.

Provide a willingness rating for each action on a scale of 1 to 5, 1: lowest and 5: highest, 1: very low willingness, 2: low willingness, 3: moderate willingness, 4: high willingness, 5: very high willingness.

Actions	Desire rating	Acceptable loss		
		What will I lose? (How much?)	Affordability rating	Willingness rating
1.		Time Money Professional reputation Personal reputation Opportunity Other		

(Continued)

(*Continued*)

Actions	Desire rating	Acceptable loss		
		What will I lose? (How much?)	**Affordability rating**	**Willingness rating**
2.		Time Money Professional reputation Personal reputation Opportunity Other		
3.		Time Money Professional reputation Personal reputation Opportunity Other		

Step 3: Select the best action

The next step is to select the best action from the list of three. Most likely, you select the one with the highest desire rating and high acceptable loss.

Step 4: People to bring along

Once you select an action to take, decide which people to bring along. It is not necessary, but it will help you gain more resources to draw on, spread the risk, enable creativity, and seek confirmation or a second opinion. Make a list of people whom you like to get in. Write what you expect from each of them. Will you empower them? How much? Use the empowerment rating E1 to E5.

Action you will take: _____		
People to bring along	What do you expect from them?	Empowerment (E1 to E5)
1.		
2.		
3.		
...		
n.		

Step 5: Reflections

Write the reflections or any lessons learned and experience built (learn–build) from the last action.

Action you will take: _____			Learn–build from the last action
People to bring along	What do you expect from them?	Empowerment (E1 to E5)	
1.			
2.			
3.			
…			
n.			

Step 6: Act

Act. Remember without actions nothing happens.

Step 7: Evaluating outcome

The outcome can be desirable or undesirable. Both give you new information, new evidence, and new insights that your competition does not have. Use the following sheet for evaluations:

Desirable outcome: (what was the outcome?)
How much was the actual loss?   How did the people feel? Would more people join?   What new evidence or insights do you have?   What is the follow-up action?   How can you do it better?   What did you learn–build?
Undesirable outcome: (what was the outcome?)
How much was the actual loss?   How did the people feel?   What new evidence or insights do you have?   What went wrong? How could you have done it better?   What did you learn–build?

In case of a predictable environment, use the following sheet:

Actions/ deliverables	Status	Target completion date	Actual completion date	Person responsible	Issues/ challenges	Remarks
1.						
2.						
3.						
...						
n.						

Fast Execution Applications

Fast execution can be applied to different areas such as customer engagement, innovations, and cultural transformation.

1. Customer Engagement

In certain situations, the customers have a clear strategy, targets, and a good understanding of market trends. They know what they want and have clear expectations from the vendors. You can use the build–act–learn model to help your customers achieve their objectives.

You must:

- Develop a plan of action with the customer.
- Deliver as per the plan.
- Have governance, reviews, and check-ins.

You can use the following sheet (add more questions if needed):

Build	Act	Learn
What specific actions will you take?	What issues and challenges did you face during the delivery?	What lessons did we learn?
In how much time?		How can we do better?
What are the risks?		
Do you have any insights to offer?		Are there any new insights to be shared?

In uncertain situations, the customers might be apprehensive to take action, due to lack of knowledge and experience. They may not even know what their needs are. You, as their trusted partner, can support them using the act–learn–build model.

Their needs may not be fully developed, and they may not be able to express their problems explicitly. They would often express their concerns through dissatisfaction statements such as:

Oh! This is working too slow.
I wish this could be more user-friendly.
Your systems are slow as compared to other vendors.

You must:

- Listen to their dissatisfactions.
- Uncover their needs.

Initially, the customer needs are hidden and unclear. Once they get clearer, they can be converted into wants, which will enable them to make clear problem statements. They need to be uncovered with the right kind of questions. Neil Rackham, the founder of Huthwaite International, developed a SPIN methodology to uncover customer needs. SPIN is an abbreviation for the kinds of questions to be asked.[4]

S: Situation questions—about the customer's current situation. For example:

- What are you doing now?
- How often do you need to stop production to maintain your equipment?
- How many people work on that machine?
- What is their average pay rate?

P: Problem questions—about customer's difficulties or dissatisfactions.

For example:

- What is the cause of machine's high downtime?
- How long does it take for maintenance to get the machine back online?
- Are there any other problems related to machine downtime?

I: Implication questions—about the consequences or implications of customer's problems.
For example:

- How does this impact your clients?
- What do your clients do when you can't deliver what they need?
- How much does this cost you when you lose production?
- Have you lost orders to competitors?

N: Need payoff questions—that explore the importance of solving a problem for the customer.
For example:

- How would your results change if you didn't have to shut down your machine?
- How would your relationship with your clients change?
- Who else would benefit from this change if it was possible?

Use the following sheet (add more questions if needed)

Act	Learn	Build
What dissatisfaction statements is the customer making?	Were you able to uncover customer needs?	How would you make your further engagements/meetings better?
How dissatisfied is the customer?	What more did you learn about the customer?	
What is your strategy for engaging with the customer?	Did you generate any insights?	
What SPIN questions will you ask?		

2. Innovations

A digital leader must be open to new ideas and innovate continuously. Figure 5.8 shows the four stages or the four *Is* of innovation[5]: ideation, initiation, incubation, and introduction.

Figure 5.8 I's of innovation

At the *ideation* stage, your idea is only at a conceptual level. There are many unknown factors such as feasibility, time, costs, risks, and so on. You might brainstorm with your team and nurture it further to the next stage.

At the *initiation* stage, your idea is backed up by a proof of concept, pilot, or feedback from your idea supporters. You have some evidence that your idea can work in a certain scenario or a use case. You lack evidence from multiple scenarios or use cases. This stage involves deep dives, experimentation, detailed analysis, and workshops with your team.

At the *incubation* stage, you develop a prototype or a minimum viable product (MVP). You identify a small, focused group of customers and develop the prototype as per their needs and requirements. This stage involves market research, staging trials, preparing business cases, and gathering feedback from early adopters.

At the *introduction* stage, your prototype develops into version 1.0 of a product or a service. It is ready to be introduced into the market, catering needs of a smaller customer base. This stage involves preparing a go-to-market strategy, calculating a marketing budget, creating an internal team, and securing feedback from customers.

Innovations have a higher element of unpredictability. You can use the act–learn–build model at every stage of the innovation process using the following sheet:

Stage		Act	Learn (What do you learn from it?)	Build (How does it help build your experience?)
Ideation	1.			
	2.			
	...			
	n.			
Initiation	1.			
	2.			
	...			
	n.			
Incubation	1.			
	2.			
	...			
	n.			
Introduc- tion	1.			
	2.			
	...			
	n.			

For every stage, under Act, write down all the actions you will take. Next to each action, under Learn, write down all the key learnings from it. And under Build, write how it helps in building your experience.

3. Cultural Transformation

To support digital transformation, it is important to create a cultural transformation in an organization that facilitates an environment of continuous learning and development (L&D) where:

- An individual takes one's own learning responsibility.
- Learning is a natural habit for individuals and teams.
- L&D is the top management priority.

- The management motivates and encourages people to learn and ensures there is a clear L&D plan for everyone.
- The company invests in the latest digital learning tools.
- There are regular check-ins and governance procedures in place.

To establish a learning culture, we make sure we:

a. Encourage and motivate people to learn

b. Develop a clear learning plan or pathway for everyone

c. Access the latest digital learning tools

d. Establish a continuous learning check-in process

e. Set up an L&D governance at all levels in your organization

Use the following sheet to implement the preceding five objectives using the act–learn–build model:

Objectives	Act	Learn (What do you learn from it?)	Build (How does it help build your experience?)
Encourage and motivate people to learn	1.		
	2.		
	...		
	n.		
Develop a clear learning plan or pathway for everyone	1.		
	2.		
	...		
	n.		
Access the latest digital learning tools	1.		
	2.		
	...		
	n.		
Establish a continuous learning check-in process	1.		
	2.		
	...		
	n.		

(Continued)

(*Continued*)

Objectives	Act	Learn (What do you learn from it?)	Build (How does it help build your experience?)
Set up an L&D governance at all levels in your organization	1.		
	2.		
	...		
	n.		

For every objective, under Act, write down all the actions you will take. Next to each action, under Learn, write down all the key learnings from it. And under Build, write how it helps in building your experience.

Summary

- Fast execution is the ability of a leader to take rapid actions in both predictable and unpredictable environments.
- In unpredictable environments, the competence, confidence, and credibility levels among people drop down.
- In unpredictable environments, use the act–learn–build model.
- In predictable environments, use the build–act–learn model.
- A leader can either fast execute himself/herself or empower people to take quick actions.
- Fast execution can be applied to different areas such as customer engagement, innovations, and cultural transformation.

CHAPTER 6

Practical Application of Frameworks

This chapter contains the practical application of the frameworks for leadership brand, growth mindset, empathy, informed decision-making, and fast execution. It can give readers a better understanding of how to apply the frameworks at the workplace, which is the main purpose of this book.

Cultivating Leadership Brand

Hardik (name changed) became the CEO of a Mumbai based mid-sized firm developing enterprise resource planning (ERP) software for small and mid-sized enterprises. The ERP product incorporated digital technologies such as AI, data analytics, and cloud. He wanted to be perceived as a digital leader to resonate with the company's progressive *digital* vision and mission. I asked him to complete the assessment. Following was the response:

Step 1: Assessing your leadership style

#	Statements	Scoring
	Section 1	
1	I always tell my subordinates/direct reports exactly what to do.	3
2	I always speak my mind without considering much how other people feel.	2
3	I am driven by a quest for unique achievements.	2
4	I make quick decisions.	1
5	I seldom involve my subordinates in decision-making.	3
6	I execute my decisions fast.	2
7	I am very result-oriented.	1

(Continued)

(Continued)

#	Statements	Scoring
	Section 1	
8	I do not like it when my team disagrees with my views.	2
9	I like to closely supervise my team.	1
10	I seldom coach or mentor my team.	2
	Total score	19
	Section 2	
11	I connect very well with my team.	3
12	I genuinely care about my team.	3
13	I openly share my thoughts and feelings with my team and expect them to do the same.	4
14	I always consider how my decision would make other people feel.	3
15	My team feels very comfortable with me.	4
16	I have a large and wide professional network.	3
17	I do not like to micromanage my team.	4
18	I am good at influencing people.	3
19	I am very receptive to change.	4
20	I am open to new ideas and suggestions from my team.	3
	Total score	34
	Section 3	
21	I strongly believe in teamwork and collaboration.	2
22	I seek my team's views and perspectives before making a decision.	3
23	I am open to people challenging my views.	2
24	I facilitate knowledge sharing with my team.	2
25	I recognize people for their contributions.	2
26	I offer feedback to people when they make mistakes.	2
27	I give everyone in my team an opportunity to participate and speak during the meetings.	2
28	I often keep people engaged at work.	2
29	My team feels their voices and opinions are heard.	2
30	My team often feels motivated at work.	2
	Total score	21
	Section 4	
31	I often delegate tasks to my team.	3
32	I have a high trust and confidence in my team.	2
33	I seldom follow up with my team after I delegate a task to them.	2

#	Statements	Scoring
	Section 4	
34	I empower people.	3
35	I seldom tell my team what to do.	2
36	I believe that freedom and autonomy are the best team motivators.	3
37	I am good at identifying my team's skills and talents.	2
38	I seldom offer any feedback to my team.	3
39	I strive to offer a good work–life balance to my team.	2
40	I take full responsibility when my team makes a mistake in executing a task.	2
	Total score	24
	Section 5	
41	I exemplify good leadership.	3
42	I set high standards of work.	2
43	I set high expectations for my team.	2
44	I often keep my team motivated.	4
45	I have good knowledge and expertise in the area of my work.	3
46	My team often seeks my advice and consultation when faced with issues.	2
47	I often do things quickly.	2
48	I often do things accurately.	3
49	I often accomplish my targets and goals.	4
50	I provide constant feedback to my team.	2
	Total score	27
	Section 6	
51	I offer constant support to my team to complete a task.	2
52	I am always available whenever my team needs me.	3
53	I like to develop and coach people.	1
54	I generally encourage the team to come up with their own solutions to problems.	2
55	I believe more in execution than planning.	3
56	I like to cultivate future leaders for my organization.	1
57	I bring out the best in my team.	2
58	I often share my knowledge and experience with my team.	2
59	My team is seldom demotivated.	2
60	I believe feedback is important for my team's development.	3
	Total score	21

Primary dominant leadership style: Affiliative

Secondary dominant leadership style: Pacesetting

Step 2: Building a leadership brand

1. Developing self-awareness
2. Assessing personal core values
3. Assessing changing organization needs

1. Developing self-awareness

Reflect

Complete the following assessment containing 24 behavior statements. Based on to what extent you agree or disagree, provide a score for each of them on a scale of 1 to 5, 1: seldom, 2: rarely, 3: sometimes, 4: often, 5: always.

Hardik's response

#	Behavior statements	Score
1	I have a clear understanding of customer business.	4
2	I can effectively translate customer needs into solutions.	4
3	I can put into perspective how my work relates to customer success.	4
4	I continuously seek feedback from customers to identify improvement.	2
5	I establish clear, realistic timelines for goal accomplishment.	3
6	I establish methods for monitoring and measuring progress.	5
7	I track performance against customer requirements.	3
8	I foster a sense of urgency in others to achieve goals.	4
9	I facilitate the team activities effectively.	3
10	I intervene appropriately to resolve conflict.	4
11	I support useful changes and identify ways to improve the efficiency of future work.	3
12	I work productively in the face of ambiguity or uncertainty.	3
13	I demonstrate a good understanding of my organization's vision, mission, and strategy.	3
14	I encourage others to look at problems and processes in new ways.	2
15	I routinely try out new methods, processes, and technologies.	1

#	Behavior statements	Score
16	I leverage ideas from others and evaluate them to ensure business viability.	2
17	I make accurate evaluations of people's capabilities and fit.	3
18	I share credit and give visibility to others.	3
19	I relate well to a variety of people regardless of their level or background.	2
20	I stand behind the decisions of the organization, superiors, or team.	4
21	I share information and viewpoints openly and directly with others.	2
22	I demonstrate an interest in people and their growth and development.	2
23	I apply and seek out the knowledge and expertise of others.	3
24	I adopt best practices and lessons learned from within and outside the organization.	2

Seek

The following was the combined score based on feedback from nine different stakeholders: two customers, six direct reports, and one peer CEO from a partner company.

#	Behavior statements	Score
1	Demonstrates a clear understanding of customer business.	3
2	Can effectively translate customer needs into solutions.	2
3	Has a good understanding of how work relates to customer success.	2
4	Continuously seeks feedback from customers to identify improvement.	1
5	Establishes clear, realistic timelines for goal accomplishment.	2
6	Establishes methods for monitoring and measuring progress.	3
7	Tracks performance against customer requirements.	Not observed
8	Fosters a sense of urgency in others to achieve goals.	3
9	Facilitates team activities effectively.	4
10	Resolves conflicts within the team.	2
11	Supports useful changes and identifies ways to improve the efficiency of future work.	Not observed
12	Works productively in the face of ambiguity or uncertainty.	Not observed
13	Demonstrates a good understanding of the organization's vision, mission, and strategy.	1

(Continued)

(*Continued*)

#	Behavior statements	Score
14	Encourages others to look at problems and processes in new ways.	3
15	Tries out new methods, processes, and technologies.	4
16	Seeks ideas from others and evaluates them to ensure business viability.	3
17	Makes accurate evaluations of people's capabilities and fit.	2
18	Shares credit and gives visibility to others.	2
19	Relates well to a variety of people regardless of their level or background.	4
20	Supports the decisions of the organization, superiors, or team.	2
21	Shares information and viewpoints openly and directly with others.	1
22	Demonstrates an interest in people and their growth and development.	1
23	Leverages the knowledge and expertise of others.	1
24	Adopts best practices and lessons learned from within and outside the organization.	Not observed

Compare the scores:

Behaviors	Reflect score	Seek score	Score difference
1	4	3	1
2	4	2	2
3	4	2	2
4	2	1	1
5	3	2	1
6	5	3	2
7	3	Not observed	NA
8	4	3	1
9	3	4	1
10	4	2	2
11	3	Not observed	NA
12	3	Not observed	NA
13	3	1	2
14	2	3	1
15	1	4	3
16	2	3	1
17	3	2	1
18	3	2	1
19	2	4	2
20	4	2	2

Behaviors	Reflect score	Seek score	Score difference
21	2	1	1
22	2	1	1
23	3	1	2
24	2	Not observed	NA

Conquer

Arena	Blind spots
Behavior statements: 1, 4, 5, 8, 9, 14, 16, 17, 18, 21, 22	Behavior statements: 2, 3, 6, 10, 13, 15, 19, 20, 23
Mask	**Unconscious**
Behavior statements: 7, 11, 12, 24	Excluded

2. Assessing personal core values

Following was Hardik's response:

1. Who is the person I respect most in life? What are their core values? My father. Commitment, professionalism, integrity.	2. Who is my best friend, and what are his/her top three qualities? Priyesh. Self-confidence, communication skills, personality.
3. If I could have more of any one quality instantly, what would it be? Communication skills.	4. What are three things I hate? Not honoring time commitments, procrastination, poor quality of work.
5. Which three people in the world do I dislike the most, and why? I mostly dislike the politicians for their hypocrisy.	6. Which personality trait, attribute, or quality do people compliment me with the most? Professionalism.
7. What are the three most important values I want to pass on to my children? The same I like in my father. Commitment, professionalism, integrity.	8. If I were to teach a graduating high-school class values that would give them the best opportunity for success in life, what would those be, and why? Professionalism—you become good at work, commitment—you deliver on time, integrity—people trust and believe in you.
9. If I had enough money to retire tomorrow, what values would I continue to hold? Integrity and commitment.	10. What values do I see being valid 100 years from now? Professionalism, commitment, integrity.

Now look at your answers. Do you notice any reoccurring themes? Considering what you've observed in others, what others have observed about you, what you want from others, and things you would fight for or against, create a list of your top 10 values or even fewer (in any order) in the following table:

#	Top values
1	Professionalism x
2	Commitment x
3	Integrity x
4	Self-confidence
5	Communication skills
6	Personality
7	
8	
9	
10	

You must shortlist six. Put *x* next to the values you're sure about. Then take the ones you feel are important but aren't sure if they are top six material, and put them in pairs. Think about two of those values side by side and ask yourself which of the two is more important, eliminating the other. Keep pitting the survivors against each other until you're down to six. If some of the values you listed are just two words describing the same idea, combine them.

List your top six values in the following table prioritized in the order of importance.

#	Top values
1	Professionalism
2	Commitment
3	Integrity
4	Communication skills
5	Self-confidence
6	Personality

Consider two values at a time and try to choose which would you fight for, or even die defending. Select the top three values.

My top three values in life are as follows:

1. Professionalism
2. Commitment
3. Integrity

3. Assessing changing organization needs

Hardik's response:

1. What are the key strengths of my organization? Robust product, customer loyalty, problem-solving.	2. What are the top challenges and pain points for my organization? Attrition, competence, marketing.
3. What are the new business opportunities for my organization? Cloud, AI, data analytics.	4. What are the threats to our business? Disruption from digital startups.
5. How is my organization better than my competitors? Customer loyalty.	6. How are my competitors better than my organization? Problem-solving, pricing, good competence.
7. What are the things that customers like about my business? Continuous product support, quality delivery.	8. What are the things that customers dislike about my business? Attrition, delays.
9. What are the things that employees like working in my organization? An opportunity to learn the ERP product, job stability.	10. What are the things that employees dislike working in my organization? Low salary, politics.
11. Is the company's value proposition well understood by the employees? Yes.	12. Is the company's value proposition well understood by the customers? Yes.
13. Does the company have a clear and concrete strategy? Somewhat yes.	14. Do the employees understand and relate to the strategy? Somewhat no.

Now, take a look at your answers. Are you able to identify some reoccurring needs? Make a list of the top 10 or fewer needs (in any order) in the following table:

#	Top needs
1	Employee retention x
2	Improve marketing x
3	Enhance employee competence x
4	Develop product further as per customer requirements x
5	Improve customer loyalty x
6	Better problem-solving
7	Improve salary
8	Remove politics
9	Improve product pricing
10	Explore new business opportunities x

You must shortlist six. Put *x* next to the needs that you are sure about. Then take the ones you feel are important but aren't sure if they are top six needs and put them in pairs. Think about two of those needs side by side and ask yourself which of the two is more important, eliminating the other. Keep pitting the survivors against each other until you're down to six. If some of the needs you listed are just two words describing the same idea, combine them.

List your top six needs in the following table:

#	Top needs
1	Employee retention
2	Improve marketing
3	Enhance employee competence
4	Develop product further as per customer requirements
5	Improve customer loyalty
6	Explore new business opportunities

Consider two needs at a time and try to choose the most urgent and important for your business having a huge impact on it. Select the top three needs.

The top three organizational needs are as follows:

1. Explore new business opportunities
2. Employee retention
3. Enhance employee competence

Leadership brand statement

Based on observations and data collected from the preceding three assessments, Hardik developed the following leadership brand statement:

I am an affiliative digital leader believing in offering improved customer loyalty through professionalism, commitment, and integrity by exploring new business opportunities and enhancing competence.

Cultivating Growth Mindset

One evening, I received a phone call from Vrinda saying that she needed my guidance in learning. I explained to her how cultivating a growth mindset enables learning and gave her the growth mindset assessment to begin with.

Following was her response:

#	Statements	Rating
1	I can take up any role at my firm.	2
2	I always make time from my daily routine to learn new skills and concepts.	2
3	Talent is not natural; it needs to be developed.	3
4	It is ok to make mistakes.	3
5	I learn best only when I make mistakes.	2
6	Hard work eventually pays off.	4
7	Every day I get better and better at my work.	3
8	I take efforts to develop people.	3
9	I don't get frustrated when things don't happen my way.	3
10	Better spend time on a difficult problem than skip it.	3
11	In case of a failed decision, I don't blame others.	4
12	I don't get annoyed when people give me negative feedback.	3
13	I overcome my weaknesses.	4
14	I don't get upset when corrected by my juniors.	3

(Continued)

(Continued)

#	Statements	Rating
15	I don't feel envious when my coworkers get promoted.	4
16	I don't feel threatened by my peers.	3
17	I often share credit with others for success.	2
18	Failures don't make me upset.	2
19	I don't feel more stressed in uncertain situations.	2
20	How things are done matters to me more than what needs to be done.	4
	Average score	2.95

Result: low growth mindset

First, I gave her information on the characteristics and behaviors of a person with a growth mindset. Then, I gave her the belief–actions–focus sheet to fill in.

Following was her response:

Belief

Why do you want to do it?

Ans: To enhance my confidence in learning new skills and feel proud of myself.

What is the benefit of doing it?

Ans: It will provide me with knowledge and enable me to engage better with customers.

What is the disadvantage of not doing it?

Ans: It will not allow me to explore new opportunities and grow.

How strongly you believe you can do it? Rate your belief on a scale of 1 to 10 (1: lowest, 10: highest)

Ans: My belief rating is 7.

Actions

What specific actions will you take?

Ans: I will dedicate two hours from my daily schedule to learn cloud. It could be an hour in the morning before or an hour in the evening after core business hours. I would like to join data analytics learning communities and forums where people share their knowledge and experiences. I would like to have a weekly follow-up with Amit (myself) to seek guidance and motivation.

What challenges are you likely to face?

Ans: Finding the time and understanding the technicalities of cloud would be two major challenges. But with dedication and a strong will, I would be able to overcome them.

How strong is your commitment level to taking action? Rate on a scale of 1 to 10 (1: lowest, 10: highest)

Ans: I am highly committed. I give all my actions a rating of 9.

Focus

How would you monitor your progress?

Ans: I will track my progress weekly. I will prepare a three-month plan, where I will make a list of all the tasks to be completed per week.

What specific KPIs would you like to introduce?

Ans: #Number of actions completed current week, #My confidence level (on a scale of 1 to 10, 1: lowest and 10: highest), #My readiness level for data analytics certification exam (on a scale of 1 to 10, 1: lowest and 10: highest).

New skills	Belief rating	Actions to be taken	Commitment rating	KPIs
Develop skills in data analytics and understand the business impact	7	Dedicate daily 2 hours for learning	9	#Number of actions completed current week
		Join learning communities	9	
		Seek help and coaching from Amit (myself)	9	#My confidence level
				# My exam readiness level

Cultivating Empathy

You must be wondering what happened to Goran. For a month, he was on bench and did not have any projects. But then, he found a project on cloud strategy and migration, the one that he was eagerly looking for. The clients were happy with his performance and his project was extended for a year. Alisa got the promotion she wanted. She was happy, but people were not happy working with her.

Alisa attended one of my *Lunch and Learn* talks at her office, where I was speaking about the importance of empathy at the workplace. At the end of the presentation, she asked me if I could help her improve and cultivate empathy.

I asked her, "Why do you want to develop empathy?"

She replied:

> I have a high attrition in my team. Many people have left the OSS legacy project over the last few months. I had a talk with HR about the situation. I got feedback that people leave because of lack of support from the manager (me).

"What is that you want to achieve from being more empathetic? Do you want to build your team, improve relationships with stakeholders, network better, mentor/reverse mentor, or anything else?" I asked.

Alisa replied, "Team building is my top priority."

We agreed to start the 12-week empathy-building program, the following week. I made her do the empathy assessment to assess her empathy level. Following was the response:

#	Statements	Rating
1	More than laying people off, it is important how you lay them off.	3
2	I often tend to listen more than I speak.	1
3	I like developing people.	1
4	I often share credit with others for success.	3
5	I am better at influencing people at work.	3
6	I get influenced by great people easily.	2
7	I manage my stakeholder relationships effectively.	3
8	I spend lots of time and effort in building my professional network.	2
9	I feel uncomfortable when one of my team members feels demotivated at work.	2
10	Before giving negative feedback to someone at work, I try to imagine how I would feel if I were in their place.	2

#	Statements	Rating
11	I know what motivates my team and how to motivate them.	2
12	I cannot tolerate disrespectful behavior in the workplace.	3
13	I share other's motivation and enthusiasm.	3
14	I feel bad when deserving employees don't get what they deserve.	1
15	I can easily understand other's views and perspectives.	3
16	I still seek input and opinions from others, even though I know the solution to a problem.	1
17	I like to help my colleagues at work.	3
18	I like to work in a team.	3
19	I deliver on commitments.	5
20	I value mine and other people's time.	5
	Average score	2.55

Empathy rating: low

Then, I asked her to come up with a list of people whom she wanted to empathize with. She came up with the names of her two assistant project managers: Karan and Petri.

She did the think–feel–will analysis for them. Following were her responses:

Data	Person 1	Person 2
Name of the person	Karan	Petri
Gender	Male	Male
Title	Assistant project manager	Assistant project manager
Number of years in the company	7	4
Working relation to you (direct report, customer, manager, executive, etc.)	Direct report	Direct report
What is the environment in which you interact (office, remote, hybrid)?	Remote	Remote
What type does the person belong to (type 1, 2, 3, 4, or 5)?	Type 3	Type 4

(Continued)

(Continued)

Data	Person 1	Person 2
As per the 4D model, how do you categorize the person?	Doer	Designer
Why do you want to empathize with the person?	To make him more motivated to take ownership of tasks.	To make him more motivated and be a part of the solution design team for the client account.
How important is the relationship to you?	Karan has domain knowledge and good people management skills. He is liked by the customers too. He is a crucial resource on my team.	Petri does not have as strong domain knowledge as Karan. However, he is a problem solver, innovative, and often develops new solutions and ways of working. He has good people skills and likes to work in a team.
What positive impact would it have on your business?	To find a replacement for him would be difficult. It can hinder our delivery to the client severely.	He has been on the project for 2 years and knows the client business well. It will have some impact but not as high as Karan.
How can you mutually benefit from each other?	If he is motivated, he can win more business as he has a good relationship with clients. I can help him with his career development, coach him, and put forward his case for promotion to management.	He can win more business by bringing innovative solutions for clients. I can help him with his career development, coach him, and put forward his case for promotion to management.

Questions	Karan	Petri
Think		
What is the person thinking about the project?	He wants to move to another one.	He seems to be liking the project.
What is the person's perspective about me?	That I am a result-oriented person.	That I am a result-oriented person.
What is the person's perspective about other people?	People on the team are talented.	People on the team are talented.
Does the person have an opinion?	Karan strongly believes that some of the tools need to be retired by the client.	Not sure. Might have one.

Questions	Karan	Petri
Will the person's perspective about the project change after we have an open dialogue?	He should be able to appreciate the value of this project to win further business from the client.	I am still unable to understand what he thinks about the project. Maybe an open dialogue will help.
Will the person's perspective about me change after we have an open dialogue?	He should be able to understand me better.	He should be able to understand me better.
Will the person's perspective about other people change after we have an open dialogue?	He should be able to connect better with his team.	I don't think it would make any difference. He is good at working with people.

Questions	Karan	Petri
Feel		
What is the person feeling about the project?	He feels this project is not helping him grow in his career.	He seems to be feeling good about the project.
How does the person feel about me (good, bad, or neutral feelings)?	Neutral	Good
How does the person feel about other people (good, bad, or neutral feelings)?	Neutral	Good
Will the person's feelings about the project change after we have an open dialogue?	Chances are less but I will try.	They might continue to remain the same.
Will the person's feelings about me change after we have an open dialogue?	Yes, he might start feeling that I am here to help him.	They might continue to remain the same.
Will the person's feelings about other people change after we have an open dialogue?	Yes, he would feel more respectful and caring toward his team.	They might continue to remain the same.

Questions	Karan	Petri
Will		
What does the person need from the project?	Expects this project to open new career doors	Needs his ideas to be more accepted
What does the person need from me?	To be more supportive	To be more supportive

(Continued)

(*Continued*)

Questions	Karan	Petri
What does the person need from other people?	To ramp up technical competence	To share more knowledge and ideas
Will the person's needs from the project change after we have an open dialogue?	No. But he might share some new needs, which I don't know.	I don't think so.
Will the person's needs from me change after we have an open dialogue?	No. But his needs can get stronger and more urgent.	I don't think so.
Will the person's needs from other people change after we have an open dialogue?	No. But he can expect something more, which I am not aware of.	I don't think so.

"Thanks Alisa, for your responses. But these are just estimates." I said. "The reality might be different. You will know only when you have an open dialogue with them."

After I coached her on the use of active listening skills while conversing with people, she was ready for a meeting with Karan and Petri.

Alisa's meeting with Petri went fine. He was open and transparent with her. As his wife had a baby recently, he would not make changes to his worklife for at least a year. He had a good grip on the project, and he was fine to continue with that. He was a bit reluctant to be a part of the solution design team, as he had to work with people outside his project though it was the same client. Overall, he felt good to have a meeting with Alisa, and they agreed to have a recurrent meeting like this every two weeks.

Karan was at first skeptical about why Alisa wanted to meet him. But then, he became comfortable when he was made aware of the agenda. The meeting with Karan did not go as per expectations. He was a bit unwilling to share his feelings with her. He said he felt fine about the project, people, and about her as a manager. Alisa knew that Karan was hiding something. However, he strongly insisted that other team members should develop the OSS technical skills. They both agreed to have a check-in meeting every Friday for 15 minutes.

At my follow-up meeting with Alisa, I assured her that she needs to be more patient and focused. She should continue to follow the 12-week program to see results. It took Karan seven weeks to open up and share his feelings with her. He did not feel psychologically safe in the beginning. But as the weeks progressed, he felt safer and more comfortable. He felt that the project was adding less value to his career. He was on the project since its kick-off four years ago, even before Alisa was assigned as the project manager, and desperately needed a change. He wanted to work on digital transformation projects in the OSS domain, his area of expertise. He felt that only he on the team had a wide knowledge of OSS, which was a progress blocker for his career. The team leads should extend their knowledge in other domains of OSS, so that they can step up to take on more responsibilities.

Alisa was empathetic to Karan. Over the next week, they both worked on a six-month competence development plan for the team leads, to be driven by Karan. If he could develop a suitable replacement successfully, he would be good to exit the project. They had an open dialogue with the customer and made them aware of the risk of relying on Karan as the sole knowledgeable resource. The customers agreed to their plan too.

Following was the outcome of the 12-week empathy program:

Weeks	Empathy toward Petri (Are you able to understand the person?) (Rating 1 to 10, 1: lowest, 10: highest)	What can you do better with Petri?	Empathy toward Karan (Are you able to understand the person?) (Rating 1 to 10, 1: lowest, 10: highest)	What can you do better with Karan?
Week 1	6	Have a dialogue with him every two weeks	2	Be patient and focused.
Week 2	6		3	Try to make him feel psychologically safe.
Week 3	6		3	Have a virtual coffee chat with him.
Week 4	7		4	Make him feel psychologically safer.

(Continued)

(Continued)

Weeks	Empathy toward Petri (Are you able to understand the person?) (Rating 1 to 10, 1: lowest, 10: highest)	What can you do better with Petri?	Empathy toward Karan (Are you able to understand the person?) (Rating 1 to 10, 1: lowest, 10: highest)	What can you do better with Karan?
Week 5	7		4	I will be traveling to Karan's city this week on a business trip. Make sure we meet for lunch.
Week 6	7		5	Try to discuss more about his career goals.
Week 7	8		6	He finally shared his true feelings. Try to find out if there is more to share.
Week 8	8		6	Cancel the Friday check-in. Schedule a 45-minute meeting on Wednesday instead.
Week 9	8		6	Ask him to come up with a competence development plan for his team.
Week 10	8		7	Have open discussions about the plan with the customers.
Week 11	8		7	Continue the empathetic talks.
Week 12	8		7	Discontinue the Friday check-ins. Have a one-to-one meeting after every two weeks.

After 12 weeks, when I met Alisa, I found her happy and thankful for my support. She said, "Wish I could have been empathetic with Goran!"

I said, "Talk to him if possible. Otherwise keep him in mind if any opportunities come up for him in the future, that suit his background and interests. I am sure he would be excited to work with you again."

Cultivating Informed Decision-Making

Consider a fictitious case of David Moore, the CEO of an industrial software development company named Company X based in Europe, who was keen on launching a digital transformation program. He had received feedback from the customers that its software product was less competitive compared to other providers in the industry as it lacked some of the latest AI, automation, analytics, and cloud features. The sales have been on the decline since the last three quarters. David and his leadership team sought external advice and offered the consulting contract to one of the best global strategic consulting firms.

Company X had around 5,500 employees with operations in the following five European markets: Western Europe, Central and Eastern Europe, Mediterranean, Nordics, and United Kingdom and Ireland. Its main offering was industrial automation software, a collection of application programs, processes, methods, workflows, and functions that aid in the collection, processing, and management of information on an industrial scale. It also offered services such as integration and maintenance and support. It had a customer base in various industrial sectors such as manufacturing, designing, mining, construction, textile, chemicals, and food processing and services.

Figure 6.1 is the organizational chart of Company X:

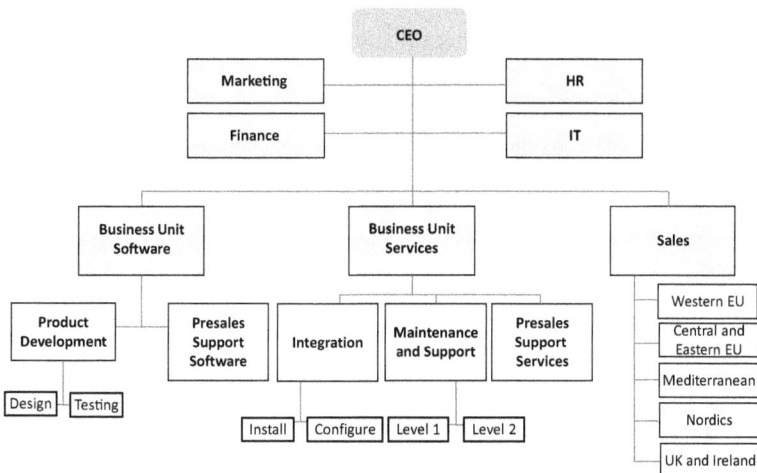

Figure 6.1 Organization chart of company X

There are two main business units: software and services. The business unit software is divided into product development and presales support software units. The product development unit comprises design and testing. The design team continuously develops new versions and features of the products, while the testing team tests them to ensure they meet the customer requirements. The presales support software team comprises the technical subject matter experts who support the sales team in selling products to the customers.

The business unit services is divided into three units: integration, maintenance and support, and presales support services. The integration team is further divided into install and configure. The install team does the installation of industrial software, and the configure team makes it go live into the customer's IT environment. The maintenance and support team provides 24/7 support to the customers by troubleshooting the issues related to the software. This unit is further divided into level 1 and level 2 support. The level 1 support team is the first point of escalation in case of any customer issues. Those that are not resolved by level 1 are escalated to level 2 team further. The presales support services unit comprises consultants, working closely with the presales support software and supporting the sales teams in selling products to the customers.

The sales unit is divided into five accounts: Western Europe, Central and Eastern Europe, Mediterranean, Nordics, and United Kingdom and Ireland, serving customers located in those specific markets. Also supporting the business, we have finance, marketing, IT, and HR units.

Following is the job structure in detail:

Jobs	Description
Business unit software	
Head of business unit software	Responsible for profit and loss of the entire unit
Product development	
Software developer	To code and develop software features and functionalities
Test engineer	To test software features and functionalities
Manager design	To lead the team of software developers
Manager testing	To lead the team of software test engineers
Director product development	To lead the product development unit

Jobs	Description
Presales support software	
System analyst	To translate customer-specific business requirements into functional requirements
Software sales support manager	Offer commercial support for software sales
Technical SME	Offer technical support during presales
Director-presales software support	To lead the presales software support unit
Business unit services	
Head of business unit services	Responsible for profit and loss of the entire unit
Integration	
Installation engineer	To install software in a customer environment
Configuration engineer	To configure and make the software go live in a customer environment
Manager install	To lead the team of installation engineers
Manager configure	To lead the team of configuration engineers
Director integration	To lead the integration unit
Maintenance and support	
Level 1 support specialist	To offer first line of support to customers
Level 2 support specialist	To offer second line of support to customers
Manager level 1 support	To lead the team of level 1 support specialists
Manager level 2 support	To lead the team of level 2 support specialists
Director maintenance and support	To lead the maintenance and support team
Presales support services	
Consultants	To offer consulting services to customers.
Service sales support manager	To offer commercial support during service sales
Director presales support services	To lead the presales support services team
Sales	
Account manager/sales director	Responsible for selling and managing relationships with new and existing customers
KAM	Profit and loss responsible for a specific customer account and lead a team of account managers and sales directors
Head of sales	Responsible for profit and loss of all the customer accounts

The consulting firm started collecting data through internal and external reports and through interviews with the unit heads and different important stakeholders. The whole activity took a month. In the end, they presented a confidential report to David, with the recommendation of a reorganization. There were few redundancies in the old organization structure with teams operating in silos. To ensure speed and agility in the ways of working, they suggested the structure with the following eight major changes proposed:

1. A new digital transformation office should be created reporting directly to the CEO. This team would be responsible for driving the digital transformation program across the company.
2. The business units: software and services would merge into a new business unit named—technology and digital business.
3. Two new teams: development and operations and centers of excellence (CoE), under the business unit technology and digital business, would be created. The development and operations would be divided into three teams: design and testing, install and config, and maintenance and support.
4. The two separate design and testing teams under product development would be merged into a new team—design and testing, comprising employees with dual competencies.
5. The two separate install and config teams under integration would be merged into a new team—install and config, comprising employees with dual competencies.
6. L2 maintenance and support would be under development and operations.
7. There would be four CoEs: AI and automation, cloud, IoT, and data science. They would be an important bridge between the customer engagements and development and operations.
8. There would be a new unit established named customer engagements, which would comprise sales, presales, marketing, level 1 support, and digital consulting. These teams would work closely to add speed and agility. The sales would continue to be driven across the five markets. The two separate presales software and presales services teams would merge as one presales team. Level 1 support team from maintenance and support would be moved under customer engagements. The marketing team would be moved from group to customer engagements. A new team named digital consulting would be created comprising experts in digital technologies as per the CoE.

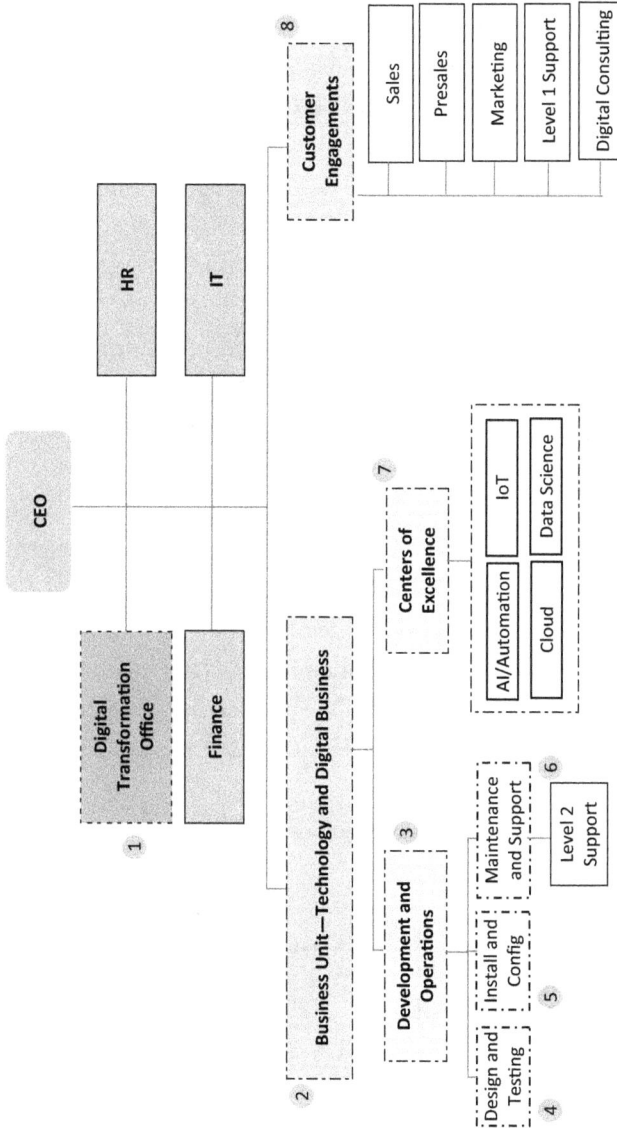

Figure 6.2 Eight major changes proposed

Following were the recommended changes to the job structure:

1. A new position head of digital transformation office to be created.
2. Heads of business units: software and services would be merged into a new position, head of business unit—technology and digital business.
3. Directors of product development, integration, and maintenance and support would be merged into director of development and operations.
4. Manager design and manager testing to be merged into manager design and testing. Manager install and manager config to be merged into manager install and config. Manager level 2 support to be reporting to the director of maintenance and support.
5. Directors of presales support software and presales support services would be merged into presales director.
6. A new position, head of customer engagements to be created. The heads of sales and marketing to be reporting to the head of customer engagements.
7. Manager level 1 support to be moved under customer engagements.
8. New positions digital consultants to be created in the digital consulting team, under customer engagements.
9. New positions: AI and automation expert, cloud expert, data science expert, Internet of things (IoT) expert, digital strategist, and business development manager to be created in the new CoE unit.

Following is the new proposed job description.

Jobs	Description
Business unit technology and digital business	
Head of business unit technology and digital business	Responsible for profit and loss of the entire unit
Development and operations	
Software specialists	To code, develop, and test software features and functionalities
Manager design and testing	To lead the team of software specialists

Jobs	Description
Integration engineer	To install the software and configure it to make it go live in the customer environment
Manager install and config	To lead the team of integration engineers
Manager level 2 support	To lead the team of level 2 support specialists
Level 2 support specialist	To offer second line of support to customers
Director product development	To lead the development and operations unit
CoE	
AI and automation expert	To provide consulting on AI and automation and serve as a link between customer engagements and development and operations
Cloud expert	To provide consulting on cloud and serve as a link between customer engagements and development and operations
Data science expert	To provide consulting on data science and serve as a link between customer engagements and development and operations
IoT expert	To provide consulting on IoT and serve as a link between customer engagements and development and operations
Digital strategist	To develop and execute a digital strategy
Business development manager	To develop new businesses with digital technologies
Head of CoE	To lead the CoEs for digital technologies
Customer engagements	
Head of customer engagements	Responsible for profit and loss of the entire unit
Sales	
Account manager/sales director	Responsible for selling and managing relationships with new and existing customers
KAM	Profit and loss responsible for a specific customer account and lead a team of account managers and sales directors
Head of sales	Responsible for profit and loss of all the customer accounts
Presales	
System analyst	To translate customer specific business requirements into functional requirements
Presales support manager	Offer commercial support for software and service sales
Technical SME	Offer technical support during presales
Director presales	To lead the presales unit

(Continued)

(Continued)

Jobs	Description
Level 1 support	
Level 1 support specialist	To offer first line of support to customers
Manager level 1 support	To lead the team of level 1 support specialists
Marketing	
Head of marketing	To lead the marketing team responsible for omni-channel product campaigns and promotions
Digital consulting	
Digital consultants	To offer consulting on digital technologies and work closely with CoE experts, business development managers, sales, and presales

The consultants gave Company X the following options for the reorganization:

1. Reduce current headcounts, ramp up internal competence.
2. Reduce current headcounts, ramp up internal competence, hire external competence.
3. Keep current headcounts, ramp up internal competence.
4. Keep current headcounts, ramp up internal competence, hire external competence.

David and his leadership team used the informed decision-making model. Following were the responses:

Define
What is the opportunity to be explored? >To prepare the organization for digital transformation by selecting the best option among the four given ones.
Rational: How much will be the revenue increase? >Ramping up internal competence will open new opportunities, which will increase revenue. Our target revenue increase is 10 to 15 percent. How much will be the cost reduction? >If we reduce our head counts by 10 percent, which is around 550, from the workforce of 5,500 approximately, the reduction in costs coming from headcounts will be 10 percent. Ramping up internal competence and hiring external competence will incur 5 to 7 percent more costs than the operational budget.

Define
Will it improve the customer experience? >Yes, using the latest digital technologies in our products and services will improve the customer experience. Are there any facts, figures, or statistics available to support decision-making? > Last year, two of our competitors underwent a reorganization to create a new operational structure to support digital transformation. One of them reduced its workforce by 7 percent and the other upskilled and reskilled its workforce, keeping the headcounts intact.
Emotional: Who are the stakeholders involved? >The executive leadership team is the key decision maker. The people impacted by the decision are the entire workforce of 5,500. What is their position? >They are in different jobs at different levels in the organization. We have a system of defining the hierarchy. We define by L1, L2, L3, L4, etc. L1 means one level below the CEO, L2 means two levels below the CEO, and so on. The headcount split is as follows: L1–7 L2–10 L3–95 L4, L5, L6–5,388 What is their level of knowledge and expertise? >The employees with technical competence are classified as beginner, intermediate, and experts. Management competence is divided into early career, mid-career, seniors, and executives. Do we need to involve additional resources? >We might need to involve L&D external consultants to seek advice on competence ramp up.
Instinctual: What is the current situation? >The official announcement of reorganization has not been made. But there are rumors circulating in the company. Most people are anxious and worried, causing an unnecessary distraction. Are there any risks involved? >We don't have experience in running transformation projects. We risk a high probability of failure. People might lose confidence and trust in us, leading to employee demotivation. Also, we haven't done a reorganization of such a large scale any time before.

(Continued)

(*Continued*)

Define
Have we explored similar opportunities in the past? >No What is our gut feeling? >We need to have a strategy and execute it well. Otherwise, there will be chaos everywhere.

Act
What is our decision? > We go with Option 4. Keep current headcounts, ramp up internal competence, and hire external competencies. Why did we make the decision? Headcount reduction might impact the morale and trust of our employees. There is a chance that many more talented people might leave us. There is a scarcity of competence in the market. Finding a suitable replacement for them might be a challenge.

Rational:

What actions will we take to explore the opportunity?
>Prepare a communication plan with the marketing team on how to communicate our decision to the employees. Have several customer workshops to seek feedback from them on how to improve our product and services with digital technologies. Plan an internal reorganization timeline. Prepare a competence development plan of action with HR.

Do we have a strategy?
>Yes, we have a digital strategy. We are a mid-sized workforce of 5,500, with around 5,200 people (94 percent) with technical competence. 6 percent of the workplace has business and management skills. Our strategy is to develop a deep technical competence in digital technologies for people with technical backgrounds and an overview of technical knowledge and its business implications for people with business and management backgrounds.

What are the costs involved?
>The transformation program would cost us around 2 million euros for 18 months.

Do we have a detailed plan of action?
>We divide our transformation into three waves of six months each. We are working on the details.

Emotional:

Do we have enough resources?
>We don't have resources with new digital technologies.

What are their expertise?
>They have expertise in the current products and legacy systems.

Act
How will we communicate with them? >We will communicate through a mass e-mail first. We will also discuss this at our quarterly all-employee meeting. How will we ensure they remain motivated? >We will motivate them with points and badges on completion of learning programs. We will have a leaderboard and provide recognition to the top 3 learners of the month. In short, we will motivate them through competition and recognition.
Instinctual: Do we have a positive feeling about our decision? >We have mixed feelings about our decision. We feel positive because we trust our people and we will work at our fullest commitment to make this transformation happen. At the same time, we feel anxious because we don't have enough competence to drive the change. Does it align with our personal values? >Our executive leadership is more people-oriented than result-oriented. Yes, our decision aligns with our personal values. Does it align with the business ethics and values? > Our corporate values are professionalism, respect, and commitment. Our decision to keep headcounts and ramp up competence aligns with it. Are we aware of the risks? >The chances of failure are 60 to 70 percent. This can lead to demotivation and turnover.
Review
(After six months, at the end of wave 1) What was the result of our decision? > Our new organizational structure became effective three months ago. We got delayed by a month. Planning and preparation took us three months. We had a monitoring period of 90 days since the new structure became effective. People are still settling into their new roles. Learning programs are being introduced for everyone. The apprehension has now been replaced by commitment and motivation.
Rational: Was the rational data helpful in decision-making? >Yes, somewhat helpful. Is the revenue improved? >No. It is too early to measure. It will take us a minimum of three years to see a return on our investments. Are the costs reduced? >No, we have managed to reduce some costs but not enough to make profits. We expect to see profits after three years.

(Continued)

(Continued)

Review
Are the customer expectations met? >Too early to measure. But we have buy-in and positive reactions from several customers.
Emotional: Was the emotional data helpful in decision-making? >Yes, to a large extent. Did the stakeholders/employees remain motivated? >Yes Were their needs met? >We have identified their needs and are in the process of fulfilling them. Do they feel their efforts were worthwhile? >Yes, we think so. That's the feedback we get from our L2 and L3 leadership. But we have an annual employee survey soon. It will communicate a much clearer picture.
Instinctual: Was the instinctual data helpful in decision-making? >Yes, to some extent What could have been done better? >Wish we had done the transformation before our competitors. It could have improved our brand perception in the market. Will you reuse this experience in future decision-making? >Yes, we have lots of lessons learned in wave 1. We will learn from our mistakes and make sure we don't repeat them in waves 2 and 3. Were we able to manage risks? >We got delayed by a month to implement the new organizational structure. We went slightly over time and budget. But we have identified our showstoppers and bottlenecks. We will manage our risks better in the upcoming waves.

Cultivating Fast Execution

Emely Hubert (name changed) was the chief learning officer at a European healthcare company with a workforce of around 5,000. She was hired with the objective of implementing a digital learning culture at the company. The existing work culture at the company was rigid with fixed and well-defined ways of working. Learning new technologies would take effort and commitment, and people were unwilling to do so. More than what to learn, people were intrigued with the question—why to learn?

She was exploring the possibilities of investing in a learning management system (LMS) platform. But she was not sure if LMS would be widely adopted and effectively utilized in the company.

Emely happened to know an ex-colleague of mine. He introduced me to her over an online meeting. The timing was perfect. I was developing a framework on fast execution and looking forward to launching a pilot. Emely agreed to be my test case.

I asked her to rate the situation on the predictability continuum. It was rated as *highly unpredictable*.

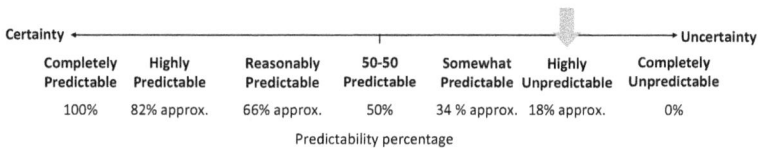

Figure 6.3 *Uncertainty continuum*

We proceeded with the act–learn–build framework.

Following was her response:

Step 1: List top 3 actions

Prepare a list of up to three actions that you would take next. Rate on a scale of 1 to 5, how strong is your desire, 1: lowest, 5: highest.

1: very low desire, 2: low desire, 3: moderate desire, 4: high desire, 5: very high desire

Actions	Desire rating (scale of 1 to 5)
1. Ask for a trial from the vendor	4
2. Secure buy-in from the leadership team	2
3. Implement an interim learning solution without an LMS	4

Following was her response to the questions:

1. Ask for a trial from the vendor.

    Why do I want to take this action?

    Ans: It will provide us with a better understanding of the product and see what feedback we get from the employees.

How important and urgent it is to take this action?

Ans: Very important and urgent.

When should I act?

Ans: I should act as soon as possible.

What exactly should I do?

Ans: I should first negotiate for a free trial. If it is not available, then try getting a good deal for a paid one.

Have I done this before?

Ans: I have done negotiations before but not for procurement of LMS.

2. Secure buy-in from the leadership team.

Why do I want to take this action?

Ans: To make sure we get the support of the leadership team in creating a learning culture.

How important and urgent it is to take this action?

Ans: Very important but not urgent.

When should I act?

Ans: At the next leadership team meeting.

What exactly should I do?

Ans: Prepare and present the solution.

Have I done this before?

Ans: Yes

3. Implement an interim learning solution without an LMS.

Why do I want to take this action?

Ans: To acquire feedback from the people with practically no costs involved.

How important and urgent it is to take this action?

Ans: Very important and urgent

When should I act?

Ans: As soon as possible.

What exactly should I do?

Ans: Use SharePoint as a repository for storing all the learning assets, start weekly knowledge-sharing sessions and collaboration forums.

Have I done this before?

Ans: Yes. I am very confident about doing this.

Step 2: Desire rating and acceptable loss

Following was her response to the desire rating and acceptable loss for each action:

Actions	Desire rating	Acceptable loss		
		What will I lose? (How much?)	Affordability rating	Willingness rating
1. Ask for a trial from the vendor	4	Time: 1 month Money: Approximately 10k Professional reputation: somewhat yes Personal reputation: NA Opportunity: yes Other: NA	Time: 3 Money: 3 Professional reputation: 2 Opportunity:2	Time: 3 Money: 2 Professional reputation:1 Opportunity: 2
2. Secure buy-in from the lead-ership team	2	Time: 1 month Money: NA Professional reputation: somewhat yes Personal reputation: NA Opportunity: yes Other: NA	Time: 3 Professional reputation: 2 Opportunity: 2	Time: 2 Professional reputation: 2 Opportunity: 2
3. Imple-ment an interim learning solution without an LMS	4	Time: NA Money: NA Professional reputation: yes Personal reputation: NA Opportunity: yes Other: NA	Professional reputation: 2 Opportunity: 2	Professional reputation: 2 Opportunity: 2

Step 3: Select the best action

Next step is to select the best action from the list of three. Most likely, you select the one with the highest desire rating and high acceptable loss.

Emely selected Option 1. Ask for a trial from the vendor.

Step 4: People to bring along

Once you select an action to take, decide which people to bring along. It is not necessary, but it will help you gain more resources to draw on, spread the risk, enable creativity, and seek confirmation or a second opinion. Make a list of people whom you like to get in. Write what you expect from each of them. Will you empower them? How much? Use the empowerment rating E1 to E5.

Action you will take: Ask for a trial from the vendor		
People to bring along	What do you expect from them?	Empowerment (E1 to E5)
1. Jan (learning programs manager)	Manage the vendor negotiations	E4

Step 5: Reflections

Write the reflections or any lessons learned and experience built (learn–build) from the last action.

Action you will take: Ask for a trial from the vendor			Learn–build from the last action
People to bring along	What do you expect from them?	Empowerment (E1 to E5)	Not applicable as this is the first action.
1. Jan	Manage the vendor negotiations	E4	

Step 6: Act

The vendor agreed to a free trial for a month.

Step 7: Evaluating outcome

The outcome was undesirable. Following was her response:

Desirable outcome: (what was the outcome?)
NA
Undesirable outcome: (what was the outcome?)
How much was the actual loss? Time: 1.5 months Money: none Professional reputation: none Personal reputation: none Opportunity: none Other: NA How did the people feel? The LMS was open to a group of early adopters of 100 people. 35 percent were eager to experiment, while 65 percent were reluctant.

What new evidence or insights do you have? Poor learning habits among the people, unwillingness to learn and experiment.
What went wrong? How could you have done it better? Out of 100 people who signed, only 5 completed the full courses. The outcome would have been better if there was a support from the leadership.
What did you learn–build? People must be motivated first to learn. Need our leaders to be the champions of learning.

"What's your next action?" I asked Emely.

"Discuss the observations with HR and the leadership team. Then most likely go for the option—Implement an interim learning solution without an LMS, if leadership is unwilling to invest." She replied.

So, what happened to Hardik, Vrinda, Alisa, and Emely?

- Hardik with his affiliative leadership style was more empathetic to the interests, needs, and concerns of his team due to which he was able to garner more respect, trust, and commitment from them. The employee attrition rate dropped by 45 percent within one year of his tenure.
- Vrinda changed her mindset from fixed to more of a growth. She changed her belief that skills can be built, and she can develop data analytics skills too. More than end results, her focus was on getting better every single day. There were challenges in learning, but she persevered through them. She valued the efforts she was putting in, which was helping her to get better. After three months of dedication and commitment, she was able to learn the basic concepts of data analytics and acquire a certification.
- Alisa changed her leadership style and became more empathetic as a leader. Besides Karan and Petri, she had open dialogues with her other team members. People are now happy and comfortable working with her.
- After having a meeting with Emely, the HR and the leadership team became aware of the employee's unwillingness to learn. They decided to address this issue urgently. Emely started taking action toward implementing the interim learning solution.

Appendix 1: Active Listening

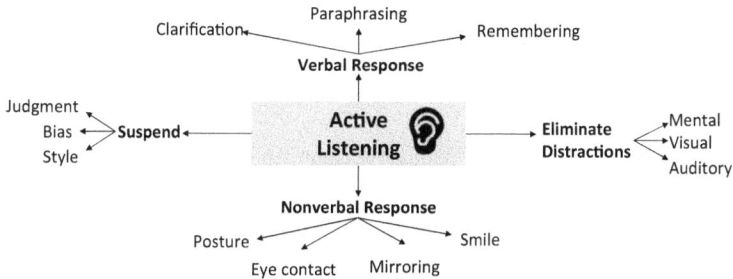

Figure A.1 Active listening model

Verbal Response

1. Paraphrasing
   Paraphrasing involves summarizing in your own words what the speaker shares with you. It is an evidence that you have heard and understood the speaker very well. It establishes rapport with the speaker and builds empathy.

2. Clarification
   Clarification usually involves the use of open questions, which requires the speaker to expand on certain points as necessary. A listener can ask for clarification when he/she cannot make sense of the speaker's responses. Sometimes, the messages a speaker is attempting to convey can be highly complex, involving many different people, issues, places, and times. Clarifying helps you to sort these out and to check the speaker's priorities.

3. Remembering
   Remembering details, ideas, and concepts from previous conversations proves that attention was kept and is likely to encourage the

speaker to continue. It can help to reinforce that the messages sent have been well received and understood. During longer exchanges, note-taking might be appropriate with the consent of the speaker.

Nonverbal Response

1. Posture

Posture can tell a lot about the sender and receiver in interpersonal interactions. The attentive listener tends to lean slightly forward or sideways while sitting. Other signs of active listening may include a slight slant of the head or resting the head on one hand.

2. Eye Contact

It is normal and usually encouraging for the listener to look at the speaker. Eye contact can however be intimidating, especially for more shy speakers—gauge how much eye contact is appropriate for any given situation. Combine eye contact with smiles and other nonverbal messages to encourage the speaker.

3. Mirroring

Automatic mirroring of any facial expressions used by the speaker can be a sign of attentive listening. These reflective expressions can help show empathy in more emotional situations.

4. Smile

Small smiles can be used to show that the listener is paying attention to what is being said or as a way of agreeing or being happy about the messages being received.

Avoid any mental, visual, or auditory distractions and suspend any bias, judgment, or style.

Appendix 2: Roleplays

You can develop your active listening skills through roleplays with your colleagues or friends.

Roleplay 1

Form a group of three and decide who will be the active listener, speaker, and observer. Think of any problem or a challenge at work or personal life that you want to speak about. The active listener should use the listening techniques. The observer should make notes to see if the active listener is employing active listening techniques. Have all three members rotate roles. Share any reflections or realizations from the roleplay.

Roleplay 2

Introduction

Form a group of three and decide who will be the manager, team member, and observer. Hand over the respective briefs to the manager and the team members. Give them five minutes to go through their respective briefs. Then, let the manager and the team member have a meeting for five minutes. Managers to be as empathetic as possible with the team members and follow the active listening principles. Observer to make notes. At the end, let both answer the following questions confidentially.

- How do I feel about the meeting?
- What do I think about the other person?
- What does the other person need from me?
- Is the other person able to understand me?
- How can the person understand me better?

At the end of the roleplay, both team member and manager share their experiences, and the observer provides feedback on the verbal and non-verbal active listening techniques.

Manager Brief

You are the manager of your team and want to have a performance appraisal meeting with one of your direct reports. This person is technically good but lacks the interpersonal skills. This will affect his overall rating as he does not demonstrate the behaviors of a team player. He is self-focused, confident about his technical skills, and does not connect well with the rest of the team. He is aspiring for a promotion. He is prompt at delivering with quality and on time. But the overall rating won't qualify him for a promotion. You do not want to lose him. If he leaves your company, it will be a loss for you. How will you tackle it?

Instructions

Be empathetic and try your best to retain and motivate your team members.

Team Member Brief

Your manager has asked you to attend the performance appraisal. You think it is a waste of time. Too much time is spent on talking rather than doing. You know that you are technically the best on the team. You desperately want a promotion and a pay raise.

Instructions

Try your best to convince your manager for at least a pay raise if not a promotion.

Roleplay 3

Introduction

Same as Roleplay 2.

Manager Brief

You are a manager of a team of 10 people, and you recently ran an innovation workshop with them where you discussed the business impact of using AI in your current product and the services you were offering to your clients. Most people contributed by sharing some ideas and knowledge. However, a senior person in the team was mostly quiet throughout the workshop and did not share much. On the contrary, he objected to certain ideas saying that they wouldn't work. You expected him to contribute, but he ended up disappointing you. Being a senior in the team, others would look upon him for directions. But his attitude might have negative implications for the team. You are a result-oriented manager who has a good knack for getting things done. You wanted to make this senior person the team lead to drive this new project of incorporating AI into the products and services. But now you are rethinking your decision. Before you take any step, you feel that you should talk to the person. What will you do?

Team Member Brief

You work in a team with a high turnover of people. You had three managers in the last 18 months. Your previous two managers had several meetings and workshops discussing new ideas. But they never implemented them. Recently, your current manager invited you to participate in an innovation workshop to discuss the business impact of AI on the products and services you were offering to your clients. You felt that these workshops would not add any value like the ones you had with your previous managers. Throughout the workshop, you were frustrated and did not participate much. In fact, you objected to the new ideas proposed by your colleagues. Another reason you kept quiet at the meeting is because of your insufficient knowledge of AI as compared to your junior team members. You were fearful about getting exposed and looking bad in front of them. You don't feel any motivation to work in the team. You are looking for new roles within your organization. But you don't want to let your current manager know as you fear it might backfire on you. Your manager wants to have a meeting with you. How will you communicate your feelings?

Conclusion

Cultivating a growth mindset, empathy, informed decision-making, and fast execution might take weeks or even months. One should start sooner and be perseverant through the development process. Taking action is important because, as seen in chapter 5, unless one takes action nothing happens.

I have experimented with these competencies on myself and on many colleagues and friends of mine who are leaders at their respective firms. They have made a remarkable impact at both personal and organizational levels. The transformation project failure rate has dropped, revenue has increased, and the customer satisfaction index has improved.

These competencies can be best developed in groups through collaboration. I want to create an ecosystem of digital leaders where one can share their experiences, best practices, challenges, and success stories in building these competencies. Please send me a connect request on LinkedIn through the profile link:

www.linkedin.com/in/amit-prabhu26/

or QR code:

And I will add you to the group.

Good leaders create good times
Good times create weak leaders
Weak leaders create tough times
Tough times create good leaders.

We see this cyclic pattern repeating over and over throughout our history: ancient, medieval, and modern. Currently, industries are going tough times. We are in the era of AI/generative AI, uncertain about its risks and implications. And the leadership is predigital; it is weak. We need good digital leaders to drive the AI transformation and create good times for everyone. It is possible through cultivation of the four key competencies: growth mindset, empathy, informed decision-making, and fast execution.

Hope you have enjoyed reading the book, as much as I have enjoyed writing it. Remember, this book is not just about Information.... It's all about *Transformation*!

Notes

Introduction

1. McKinsey (2019).
2. Tarver (2022).
3. Share Now website (n.d.).

Chapter 1

1. Cox (2022).
2. EY Press Release (2021).
3. Oracle (2023).
4. Roberts (1993), p. 1.
5. Roach (2021).
6. World Economic Forum (2023).
7. Fenlon and McEneaney (2018).
8. Smith (2022).
9. Gratton (2021), p. 4.
10. Harvard Business Review (2022), p. 3.
11. Haas (2022), p. 3.
12. Tom (2022).
13. Ulaga, Niessing and Brandwein (2019).
14. Martin (2023).
15. ASM Group Inc (2023).
16. Emeritus (2023).
17. Sridharan (2021).
18. Olmstead (2023).
19. Deslandes (2022).
20. Johari Window (n.d.).

Chapter 2

1. Page (2020).
2. Ragan (n.d.).
3. Derler, Cardero, Simpson, Grant, Slaughter, Baer, and Celi (n.d.).
4. Ibarra, Rattan, and Johnston (2018).
5. D'Orazio (2014).
6. Ibarra, Rattan, and Johnston (2018).
7. Ibid.
8. Nadella, Shaw, and Nichols (2017), p. 113.
9. Ibarra, Rattan, and Johnston (2018).
10. Ibid.

Chapter 3

1. Harvard Business Review, Goleman, McKee, and Waytz (2017), pp. 48.
2. Prabhu (2018).
3. Huy and Duke (2022).
4. Kurtuy (2023).

Chapter 4

1. Risely (n.d.).
2. PON Staff (2023).
3. Dolan (2023).
4. Hammond, Keeney, and Raiffa (2006).
5. Lobo (2021).
6. Aminov, De Smet, Jost, and Mendelsohn (2019).

Chapter 5

1. Maersk Press Release (2022).
2. Wikipedia (n.d.).
3. Website Gobito (n.d.).
4. Website Huthwaite International (n.d.).
5. Meyer (2023).

References

Aminov, I., A. de Smet, G. Jost, and D. Mendelsohn. April 20, 2019. "Decision Making in the Age of Urgency. McKinsey & Company. www.mckinsey.com/capabilities/people-and-organizational-performance/our-insights/decision-making-in-the-age-of-urgency.

ASM Group Inc. May 30, 2023. "The Power of Data: How Leveraging Insights Can Drive Business Success." www.linkedin.com/pulse/power-data-how-leveraging-insights-can-drive-business-success#:~:text=By%20leveraging%20data%20to%20make,inform%20their%20decision%2Dmaking%20processes.

Cox Guest Blogger. August 1, 2022. "A Growth Mindset: Your Organization's Strategic Differentiator." www.channelfutures.com/from-the-industry/a-growth-mindset-your-organizations-strategic-differentiator.

D'Orazio, D. February 4, 2014. "Read Satya Nadella's First Letter to Employees as Microsoft's CEO." Source Microsoft. www.theverge.com/2014/2/4/5377318/microsoft-ceo-satya-nadella-first-letter-to-employees.

Derler, A., R. Cardero, M. Simpson, H. Grant, M. Slaughter, D. Baer, and I. Celi. n.d. "Idea Report- growth Mindset culture." NeuroLeadership Institute.

Deslandes, N. September 29, 2022. "Digital Transformation Delays Cost Organizations Over £3m per Project, Research Says." https://techinformed.com/digital-transformation-delays-cost-organisations-over-3m-per-project-research-says/.

Dolan, B. May 11, 2023. "Framing Effect: What It Is and Examples." Reviewed by G. Scott, Fast checked by S. Kvilhaug. www.investopedia.com/framing-effect-7371439.

Emeritus. February 28, 2023. "The Importance of Data Analytics: How Does It Benefit a Business?" https://emeritus.org/blog/data-analytics-data-analytics-benefits/.

EY Press Release. October 14, 2021. "New EY Consulting Survey Confirms 90% of US Workers Believe Empathetic Leadership Leads to Higher Job Satisfaction and 79% Agree It Decreases Employee Turnover." www.ey.com/en_us/news/2021/09/ey-empathy-in-business-survey.

Fenlon, M. and S. McEneaney. October 15, 2018. "How We Teach Digital skills at PwC." *Harvard Business Review.*

Gratton, L. May 1, 2021. "How to Do Hybrid Right." *Harvard Business Review,* p. 4.

Haas, M. February 15, 2022. "5 Challenges of Hybrid Work- and How to Overcome Them." *Harvard Business Review,* p. 3

Hammond, J.S., R.L. Keeney, and H. Raiffa. January 1, 2006. "Hidden Traps in Decision Making." *Harvard Business Review.*

Harvard Business Review, D. Goleman, A. McKee, and A. Waytz. May 9, 2017. "Book: Empathy." *Harvard Business Review Press*, pp. 48.

Harvard Business Review. November 1, 2022. "Revitalizing Culture in the World of Hybrid Work." *Harvard Business Review*, p. 3.

Huy, Q.N. and L. Duke. December 2022. "Enhancing Innovation Through Organisational Learning and a Culture of Empathy: Microsoft under CEO Satya Nadella." INSEAD.

Ibarra, H., A. Rattan, and A. Johnston. June 2018. "Satya Nadella at Microsoft: Instilling a Growth Mindset." London Business School.

Kurtuy, A. January 4, 2023. "25+ Surprising Networking Statistics [Relevant in 2023]." https://novoresume.com/career-blog/networking-statistics#:~:text=Studies%20show%20that%20less%20than,but%20they%20have%20no%20time.

Lobo, R. March 1, 2021. "The Hidden Traps in Decision Making." www.linkedin.com/pulse/hidden-traps-decision-making-romit-lobo/.

Maersk Press Release. November 29, 2022. "A.P Moller—Maersk and IBM to Discontinue TradeLens, Blockchain-Enabled Global Trade Platform." www.maersk.com/news/articles/2022/11/29/maersk-and-ibm-to-discontinue-tradelens#:~:text=Starting%20today%2C%20the%20TradeLens%20team,without%20disruptions%20to%20their%20businesses.

Martin, C. March 22, 2023. "Gartner: Data, Analytics Investments Rising but Leaders Not Finding Value." https://aibusiness.com/data/gartner-data-analytics-investments-rising-but-leaders-not-finding-value.

McKinsey. July 10, 2019. "Why Do Most Transformations Fail? A Conversation with Harry Robinson." Video, 0:16. www.mckinsey.com/capabilities/transformation/our-insights/perspectives-on-transformation.

Meyer, R. February 1, 2023. "5I Innovation Pipeline." www.tias.edu/en/item/5i-innovation-pipeline.

Nadella, S., G. Shaw, and J. Nichols. 2017. *Hit Refresh: The Quest to discover Microsoft's Soul and Imagine a Better Future for Everyone*, p. 113. William Collins.

Olmstead, L. May 1, 2023. "The Cost of Digital Transformation in 2023." https://whatfix.com/blog/digital-transformation-cost/.

Oracle. April 19, 2023. "Global Study: 70% of Business Leaders Would Prefer a Robot to Make Their Decisions." www.prnewswire.com/news-releases/global-study-70-of-business-leaders-would-prefer-a-robot-to-make-their-decisions-301799591.html.

Page, O. November 4, 2020. "How to Leave Your Comfort Zone and Enter Your 'Growth Zone'." https://positivepsychology.com/comfort-zone/.

PON Staff. August 8, 2023. "The Anchoring Effect and How It Can Impact Your Negotiation." www.pon.harvard.edu/daily/negotiation-skills-daily/the-drawbacks-of-goals/#:~:text=2023%20%2F%20Negotiation%20Skills-, The%20anchoring%20effect%20is%20a%20cognitive%20bias%20 that%20describes%20the,information%20to%20make%20subsequent%20 judgments.

Prabhu, A. December 2018. "Business Impact of Digital Transformation Technologies." Udemy Course.

Risely. n.d. "Why Is Informed Decision-making Important for Managers?" www.risely.me/informed-decision-making-important-for-managers/#:~: text=Informed%20decision%2Dmaking%20refers%20to,and%20make %20the%20best%20choice.

Roach, L. May 7, 2021. "Embedding Speed and Agility Into Strategy Execution." https://hbr.org/sponsored/2021/05/embedding-speed-and-agility-into-strategy-execution.

Roberts, M.J. February 3, 1993. *Note on the Hiring and Selection Process*, p 1. Harvard Business School.

Share Now website. 2023. www.share-now.com/ (accessed August 10, 2023).

Smith, M. April 28, 2022. "64% of Workers Would Consider Quitting If Asked to Return to the Office Full-time." www.cnbc.com/2022/04/28/64percent-of-workers-would-consider-quitting-if-asked-to-return-to-office-full-time .html.

Sridharan, M. July 8, 2021. "Quick Wins- Power of Delivering Incremental Success." https://thinkinsights.net/consulting/quick-wins-power-of-delivering-incremental-success/#:~:text=Furthermore%2C%20early%20successes%20 can%20boost,on%20how%20people%20perceive%20you.

Tarver, E. December 22, 2022. "Corporate Culture Definition, Characteristics and Importance." Reviewed by T. Brock, fast checked by P. Rathburn. www .investopedia.com/terms/c/corporate-culture.asp (accessed August 10, 2023).

Tom, A. July 8, 2022. "How to Help Employees Connect to Their Work And Your Company." www.forbes.com/sites/forbeshumanresourcescouncil/ 2022/07/08/how-to-help-employees-connect-to-their-work-and-your-company/#:~:text=Through%20regular%20check%2Dins%2C%20 storytelling,engaged%20and%20connected%20at%20work.

Ulaga, W., J. Niessing, and N.J. Brandwein. May 2, 2019. *WeWork- Service Excellence Through Business Model Innovation: Creating Outstanding Customer Experiences by Leveraging Data, Analytics and Digital Technologies*. INSEAD.

Website Gobito. n.d. www.gobito.com/brands/akademi.

Website Huthwaite International. n.d. www.huthwaiteinternational.com/blog/complete-guide-to-spin-selling.

Wikipedia. n. d. "Public Key Infrastructure." https://en.wikipedia.org/wiki/Public_key_infrastructure.

Wikipedia. n.d. "Johari Window." https://en.wikipedia.org/wiki/Johari_window.

World Economic Forum. January 16, 2023. "5 Ways We Can Develop the Digital Skills Our Economy Needs." www.weforum.org/agenda/2023/01/5-ways-develop-digital-skills-davos2023/ (accessed August 11, 2023).

YouTube video by Ragan, T. n.d. "Growth Mindset Introduction: What It Is, How It Works, and Why It Matters." www.youtube.com/watch?v=75GFzikmRY0.

About the Author

Amit Prabhu is the author of *Digital Strategy Framework*. He has over a decade of corporate experience in global business management, strategy, and consulting. He holds a master's degree in telecommunications and networking from the University of Pennsylvania. He is also a business trainer, speaker, faculty, entrepreneur, and swimming coach. *Explorer* and *teacher* are the two words that describe him vividly. He lives in Stockholm, Sweden, with his wife and a son.

Index

Note: Page numbers followed by "f" refers to figures.

OTHER TITLES IN THE BIG DATA, BUSINESS ANALYTICS, AND SMART TECHNOLOGY COLLECTION

Mark Ferguson, University of South Carolina, Editor

- *Digital Strategy Framework* by Amit Prabhu
- *Thriving in a Data World* by Sangeeta Krishnan
- *Business Models in Emerging Technologies* by Stylianos Kampakis, Theodosis Mourouzis, Marialena Zinopoulou and Gerard Cardoso
- *Getting Data Science Done* by John Hawkins
- *Four Laws for the Artificially Intelligent* by Ian Domowitz
- *The Data Mirage* by Ruben Ugarte
- *Introduction to Business Analytics, Second Edition* by Majid Nabavi, David L. Olson and Wesley S. Boyce
- *Emerging Technologies* by Errol S. van Engelen
- *Data-Driven Business Models for the Digital Economy* by Rado Kotorov
- *Highly Effective Marketing Analytics* by Mu Hu
- *Business Analytics, Volume II* by Amar Sahay
- *New World Technologies* by Errol S. van Engelen

Concise and Applied Business Books

The Collection listed above is one of 30 business subject collections that Business Expert Press has grown to make BEP a premiere publisher of print and digital books. Our concise and applied books are for...

- Professionals and Practitioners
- Faculty who adopt our books for courses
- Librarians who know that BEP's Digital Libraries are a unique way to offer students ebooks to download, not restricted with any digital rights management
- Executive Training Course Leaders
- Business Seminar Organizers

Business Expert Press books are for anyone who needs to dig deeper on business ideas, goals, and solutions to everyday problems. Whether one print book, one ebook, or buying a digital library of 110 ebooks, we remain the affordable and smart way to be business smart. For more information, please visit www.businessexpertpress.com, or contact sales@businessexpertpress.com.

www.ingramcontent.com/pod-product-compliance
Lightning Source LLC
Chambersburg PA
CBHW061209220326
41599CB00025B/4583